Prompt Engineering for Beginners

A Comprehensive Guide

Kapila Arora

Geetu Garg

Gaurav Aroraa

ARCCHIE

www.arcchieonline.com

Prompt Engineering for Beginners
A Comprehensive Guide

KAPILA ARORA
MEERUT, INDIA

GEETU GARG
PUNE, INDIA

GAURAV ARORAA
DELHI, INDIA

Arcchie Publications has made every effort to provide trademark information about all the companies and products mentioned in this book through the appropriate use of capitals. However, Arcchie Publications cannot guarantee the accuracy of this information.

Editor: Shambhu
Production Manager: Meghna
Cover design by Freepik
Formatting & Indexing: Gaurav

First Edition: June-2024

Reference: 2309014

Published by Arcchie Publications

ISBN-13 (paperback): 978-81-966127-7-1

www.arcchieonline.com

TABLE OF CONTENTS

FOREWORD

Prompt Engineering has become more than just a skill; it is a catalyst for innovation, a muse for creativity, and a tool that empowers individuals across diverse disciplines. This book, meticulously crafted by experts in the field, serves as an inviting gateway for beginners to step into the world of prompts, unraveling its secrets and harnessing its incredible power. "Prompt Engineering for Beginners: A Comprehensive Guide" stands as a beacon for those seeking to unlock their imaginative potential and apply these techniques to build the next generation of LLM applications.

As you embark on this journey, you will immerse yourself in a comprehensive exploration of Prompt Engineering. The guide offers a perfect blend of theory and practice, walking you through the fundamental principles and gradually guiding you toward crafting compelling prompts that spark creativity and problem-solving prowess.

"Prompt Engineering for Beginners" is more than an instructional manual; it's an immersive experience. The authors seamlessly integrate practical exercises and real-world applications, providing a hands-on approach to learning. By engaging with the exercises, you will grasp the theoretical underpinnings of Prompt Engineering and experience firsthand the transformative impact it can have on your creative endeavors.

The book's relevance spans various domains, from creative writing to the boardrooms of professionals, making it a versatile companion for anyone seeking to overcome creative blocks and enhance their idea-generation skills. The insights shared by expert Prompt Engineers add a layer of wisdom, enriching the reader's understanding and offering valuable perspectives on the art and science of prompt creation.

One of the key strengths of this guide lies in its inclusivity. Tailored for beginners with no prior experience in Prompt Engineering, it serves as a gentle mentor, encouraging readers to tap into their creative reservoirs. The comprehensive introduction, step-by-step guidance, and

exploration of digital tools ensure that readers, regardless of their background, can grasp the nuances of Prompt Engineering and apply them in their respective domains.

By the end of this journey, readers will have acquired a solid understanding of Prompt Engineering and developed the skills to create thought-provoking prompts, overcome creative blocks, and apply these techniques in their endeavors. Whether you are a writer, artist, educator, student, or professional, this guide is your key to unlocking the doors of creative expression and problem-solving.

So, as you turn the pages of "Prompt Engineering for Beginners," remember that you are not just reading a book but embarking on a transformative adventure. May the prompts you create light the path to your creative zenith.

Warm Regards,

(AB) A B Vijay Kumar

IBM Fellow, Master Inventor

Global CTO Hybrid Cloud Services

GitHub/Twitter/Linkedin/Medium - @abvijaykumar

DEDICATED TO

I dedicate this book to my husband, Raman Goel, for his continuous guidance and fostering positivity and motivation.

- Kapila Arora

I want to acknowledge my son, who entered this world at a remarkable time and was born in the age of AI. I dedicate this work to him and to all who enthusiastically embrace the potential of this technology. As we navigate the complexities of this rapidly evolving field, we may all find inspiration, guidance, and the courage to push the boundaries of what is possible, shaping a future where innovation and compassion intertwine to create a world of endless possibilities.

- Geetu Garg

I want to dedicate this book to the most respectable and loveable person in my life, `Col. Inderjeet Singh`, a veteran, a Cyber Expert, an AI enthusiast, and an Inventor. A man with principles and discipline. He always admires me for doing whatever is exciting to me. This book is my gratitude for his guidance and mentorship throughout the whole journey of this book..

- Gaurav Aroraa

ACKNOWLEDGMENTS

Writing a book is a collaborative process that involves knowledge, research, continuous learning, and not just putting words together; it also requires inspiration, direction, and steadfast support. As I reflect on completing this work, I am profoundly humbled and grateful for the contributions of countless individuals and forums who have illuminated my path. I sincerely appreciate the support of my co-authors, Gaurav Aroraa and Geetu Garg. I appreciate all my leaders, mentors, and colleagues who have provided a platform, shared insights, and shaped my understanding of the subject. I am deeply humbled and grateful to my family for their extensive support. Their unwavering belief in me and constant encouragement have been the driving force behind the completion of this book.

- Kapila Arora

Reflecting upon the journey of crafting this book on prompt engineering, I am deeply grateful to my co-authors, who have supported and contributed to its completion. My heartfelt thanks go to my family for their unwavering encouragement and understanding during the countless hours spent researching and writing. I extend my appreciation to my colleagues and mentors whose insights and expertise have enriched the content of this work. Special recognition is also due to the reviewers and editors whose meticulous feedback and suggestions have helped refine its clarity and coherence. I also express gratitude to the readers whose interest in the subject fuels my passion for sharing knowledge. This book is a collaborative effort, and I am truly honored to have been supported by such an exceptional community.

- Geetu Garg

ABOUT THE AUTHORS

Kapila Arora is a Senior Certified Architect at IBM, having almost 20 years. She is a thought leader in Conversation AI, Enterprise Hybrid, and Multi-Cloud Architectures, specializing in Application Integration, Data, Infrastructure, and Government Blockchain Solutions. With extensive exposure to the end-to-end lifecycle of enterprise applications (EA), she holds a remarkable track record of architecting and delivering end-to-end solutions across various industries and global customers across geographies. She effortlessly embraces new technology with a problem-solving approach. She is an enthusiastic and clear thinker. Kapila Arora's impact extends beyond her technical expertise. She has been instrumental in leading Diversity and Women in the tech (WIT) initiatives for IBM's Financial sector. Her efforts have been recognized with the Women in the tech (WIT) award by one of the largest UK Bank Engagements. Her commitment to diversity and inclusion is further highlighted by the numerous awards and recognitions she has received throughout her journey within IBM and her previous organization. She is an active member of IBM internal communities to produce various offerings as architectural, solutions, and delivery guidance assets for Generative AI, Cloud, and Integration space.

Geetu Garg is a Senior Advisory Application Architect with over 18 years of experience in technology and works with top-notch clients in cross-industry domains. She helps organizations build and modernize their IT landscape with her expertise in Hybrid Cloud and GenAI, and she has been recognized with several awards throughout her journey.

Geetu Garg is not just a leader in technology, but also a champion for Women in Technology at IBM Consulting and IBM Financial Services. Her passion for technology is matched only by her dedication to supporting and mentoring individuals within and outside her organization. Her active involvement in external organizations and her strong reputation in technology and leadership further underscore her commitment to the industry.

ABOUT THE AUTHORS

Gaurav Aroraa is a professional with over 27 years of industry experience. His impressive achievements, including being a MuleSoft Mentor, recipient of the Microsoft MVP award, and serving as a Mentor of Change with AIM NITI Aayog, Govt. of India, speak volumes about his expertise. Gaurav is also a Business Coach with Business Blaster, Govt. of NCT of Delhi, India. He holds a lifetime membership with the Computer Society of India (CSI) and serves as an advisory member and Senior Mentor at India Mentor. He is certified as a Scrum trainer and Coach, ITIL-F certified, and holds PRINCE-F and PRINCE-P certifications. He is also a certified Microsoft Azure architect, MuleSoft Platform Architect, MuleSoft Integration Architect, and a Microsoft Certified Azure Data Scientist Associate. He has authored books on various technologies.

Gaurav recently achieved the distinction of being recognized as a World Record Holder for his exceptional book writing in various technologies. He holds 15 patents in disciplined technologies. Gaurav is passionate about sharing his knowledge and believes "sharing is caring." He actively mentors underprivileged students, and he is associated with the NGO SHIKSHA एक पहल.

You can reach Gaurav at:

Blog: *https://gaurav-arora.com/blog/*
LinkedIn: *https://linkedin.com/in/aroragaurav/*

ABOUT THE TECHNICAL REVIEWER

Siddhartha Sood is an IBM Executive Architect with two decades of vast Industry experience. He specializes in the Travel and Transportation domain. He has been advising Global Supply Chain and Airline companies on their transition to the Cloud. As an Executive Architect, Siddhartha has extensive experience in Cloud transformation, defining Enterprise Architecture, developing Technical Roadmaps, and executing Complex Transformation projects on public and hybrid clouds. He specializes in Cloud Native, Cloud Transformation, Container Technologies, Industry Solutions, Domain Driven Design, Product Engineering, Legacy Modernization, and Mainframe Modernization and has been Certified on multiple Cloud platforms. He focuses on leveraging Next-Generation Technologies such as Hybrid Cloud, AI, and Generative AI to help enterprises optimize their journey to Cloud and Software Engineering processes. Siddhartha holds ten patents and is acclaimed as an IBM Master Inventor and a member of IBM's Open Innovation Community.

ABOUT THE TECHNICAL EDITORS

Kaushal Mehta is an Associate Professor at Bhai Parmanand DSEU Shakarpur Campus-II, with over 15 years of experience in his field. His extensive knowledge and dedication to education have made him a respected figure in academia. Throughout his career, Kaushal has been committed to fostering a deep understanding of his subject matter among students and peers.

PREFACE

Recent advancements in artificial intelligence (AI), natural language processing (NLP) technology, and Generative AI (Gen AI) have led to a rapid evolution of prompt engineering, a relatively new stream.

Prompt Engineering has emerged as a transformative technique for enhancing creativity and productivity in various fields. This book provides a comprehensive and beginner-friendly introduction to Prompt Engineering, equipping readers with the knowledge and skills to harness its potential. From understanding the basics to applying advanced strategies, this guide is a steppingstone for anyone looking to excel in creative writing, problem-solving, and idea generation.

"Prompt Engineering for Beginners" is a universal resource that demystifies the world of prompt-driven creativity. Whether you're a writer, artist, educator, or professional in any field, Prompt Engineering can be your key to unlocking innovative thinking. This book delves into the core concepts of Prompt Engineering, unraveling its methodologies and techniques through practical examples and exercises. From generating ideas to overcoming creative blocks, readers will discover the power of prompts in fostering creativity and expanding their imaginative horizons.

Let's embark on this journey of learning together.

What's Inside This Book

Chapter 1: Introduction to Prompt Engineering introduces the concept of Prompt Engineering and its significance in fostering creativity and innovation. It also highlights its practical applications and discusses the role of prompts in idea generation and problem-solving.

Chapter 2: The Art and Science of Crafting Prompts delves into the process and techniques for creating effective prompts that trigger imaginative thinking.

Chapter 3: Generating Ideas Through Prompts explores how prompts can be used as catalysts for idea generation and brainstorming, emphasizes the benefits of using prompts in these processes, and explores the power of prompts.

Chapter 4: Overcoming Creative Blocks with Prompts delves into uncovering strategies to overcome creative blocks and reignite the spark of creativity using prompts. It provides detailed strategies and techniques for using prompts as tools to break through artistic and mental barriers.

Chapter 5: Applying Prompt Engineering in Writing explores how Prompt Engineering can enhance writing skills and foster originality in content creation.

Chapter 6: Exploring Visual and Artistic Prompt Techniques discovers how visual prompts can inspire artistic expression and visual storytelling.

Chapter 7: Using Prompts in Education and Training explores the role of prompts in educational contexts, how they foster critical thinking and skill development, and how they integrate into teaching and training methodologies.

Chapter 8: Digital Tools for Prompt Engineering explores various digital tools and platforms that facilitate prompt generation and management, embracing technology to streamline the prompt engineering process.

For Whom This Book Is Intended

This book is designed for:

- Novice enthusiasts seeking to explore Prompt Engineering's Potential
- Beginners who are eager to explore the world of Prompt Engineering
- Writers, artists, educators, students, and professionals seeking to enhance their creativity and problem-solving abilities.
- No prior experience in AI, Generative AI or Prompt Engineering is required.

Download the source code and colored images:

To download the source code bundle

and the colored images, please follow the link

OR

scan the QR Code

https://encr.pw/9788196612771

Errata

At **ARCCHIE Publications**, we are committed to delivering the highest-quality content in all our publications. We follow best practices to ensure the accuracy of our content to provide our readers with an indulgent reading experience. We believe and understand that our readers are our best judges, and we always use their input and feedback from time to time to improve human errors, if any, that may occur during the publishing processes involved. We invite you to participate in our errata submission process to ensure our books remain accurate and up to date. Please help us reach out to readers who might have difficulties due to unforeseen errors. Please write to us at *errata@arcchieonline.com*.

When submitting errata, please include the following information:

- Book Title
- Reference#
- Author(s)
- Page Number
- Description of the Error
- Suggested Correction (if applicable)

The **ARCCHIE Publications** Family highly appreciates your support, suggestions, and feedback.

Sharing Your Perspective and Providing Feedback

Your perspective is invaluable to us, as it helps us enhance our content and gather your feedback. We warmly welcome all forms of feedback. Please feel free to send us an email at `feedback@arcchieonline.com`, mentioning the book title in the subject line of your message.

Book Review Invitation

We kindly invite you to share your thoughts. After you've read and engaged with this book, consider leaving a review on the platform where you acquired it. Your impartial feedback can greatly assist potential readers in making informed decisions. Your reviews provide valuable insights for us at `Arcchie`, helping us better understand your perspectives on our products, and they offer authors the chance to appreciate your feedback on their work.

PIRACY

Should you encounter unauthorized reproductions of our publications in any digital format on the internet, we kindly request your assistance in pinpointing their locations or website sources. Please reach out to us at `copyright@arcchieonline.com` and include a link to the infringing material.

If you possess expertise in a particular subject and wish to participate in the creation or contribution to a book, please visit *authors.arcchieonline.com*. We welcome you and assist you to start your authorship journey with `ARCCHIE PUBLICATIONS`.

Chapter 1
Introduction to Prompt Engineering

The current era of innovation places a significant emphasis on developing novel approaches, which can help to enhance efficiency with automated operations, leveraging Artificial Intelligence (AI). AI has subset as Machine Leaning, comes under computer science. It is dedicated to crafting systems capable of emulating human thought processes and behaviors. A few examples are Siri, Alexa, and customer service chatbots which appear on various websites.

In Machine Learning, computer algorithm (model) trained on the sample dataset. These models can predict and generate the output based on provided input while provided input can be new or unseen data or partial new data. Outcome from the algorithm (model) are numbers, predictions, probability etc. Machine learning is like training a computer algorithm/model to learn from example dataset so that it can decide or predict the output based on input data on its own. Google smart reply is an example of Machine Learning.

Machine Learning has subfield as Deep learning. Deep learning uses artificial neural networks with several layers involved. These neural networks are designed to learn and understand the data like the human brain. Training data has much more unstructured or complex data than traditional Machine Learning data like images, audio, text etc. Deep learning demands vast amounts of data to drive learning and training the algorithm. Few Deep learning system examples are Facial recognition, Speech recognition etc.

Deep learning has subfield as Generative AI. Generative AI evolved with Large Language Model or Foundation Model. Large Language Models can produce or generate text/content, images, audios, blogs, code, poems etc., based on input ask. Large Language model can understand the context and semantics of the input question and is able to predict or generate the next word. Large Language Model are trained on very vast amount of data. Few Examples of Large Language Models are GPT 3, GPT 3.5, GPT 4 from Open API etc. Full Form of GPT is Generative Pre-Trained Transformer.

ChatGPT is an example of Generative AI tooling supported by OpenAI Large Language model as GPT 3, GPT 3.5, GPT 4. ChatGPT is an interface to interact with Large Language Model as GPT 3.5 and GPT 4. User, as a consumer of ChatGPT, write a prompt to enquire question to ChatGPT. Based on Input prompt, ChatGPT generates an output or response in similar context & semantic and provide back to the user on ChatGPT interface. This output generation process by Large Language model or pretrained transformer is called Generative AI. Asking a question to the ChatGPT or any other equivalent Large Language Model is called the prompting.

As described above, please find below the pictorial representation of AI and their subfields.

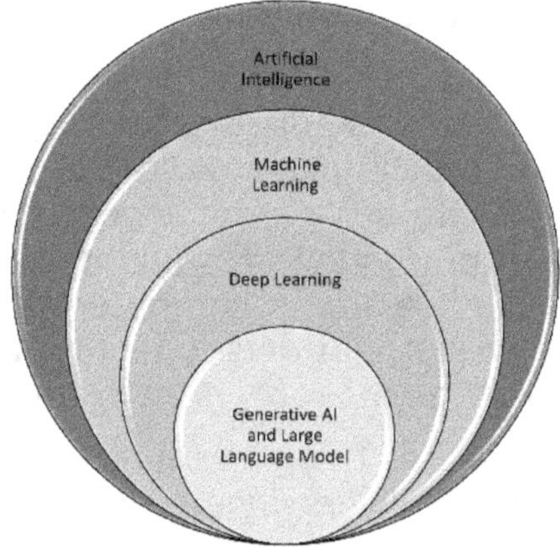

Figure 1.1: Relationship in AI, ML, DL and GenAI

I hope we now know the context of artificial intelligence (AI) , machine learning, deep learning and generative AI.

In this chapter we will cover the below topics:

- Large Language Model
- Defining Prompt Engineering
- The Benefits of Creative Prompts
- The Psychology of Prompts

> **Tip**: In simple layman's definition: Prompt as a noun like a short message or signal that tells someone what to do. In computer interfaces and communication, prompts are used to ask for a response or action; on the other hand, when you prompt someone, you're basically nudging or encouraging them to do a certain thing or give a specific answer.

Large Language Model

A class of foundation models known as large language models (LLMs). These LLMs have been trained on vast amounts of data, enabling it to comprehend and produce natural language and other kinds of content for a variety of uses.

To improve their natural language processing (NLP) and natural language understanding (NLU) capacities, numerous businesses have invested years in deploying LLMs at various levels. This has happened in advancement & developments in machine learning models, algorithms, neural networks, and transformer models—which serve as the architecture for these AI systems.

Precisely, LLM are designed to comprehend and produce writing like a human in addition to other types of content. They can translate material into languages other than English, infer from context, produce coherent and contextually relevant comments, summarize text, respond to queries (both general and FAQ-related), and even help with creative writing or code generating activities.

Microsoft, in partnership with Open AI, has endorsed interfaces such as Chat GPT-3 and GPT-4, which make LLMs readily available to the public. These interfaces mark a substantial advancement in natural language processing (NLP) and artificial intelligence (AI). While Other illustrations like Google's PaLM models and Meta's Llama models, IBM recently launched Granite model series, which is introduced on Watsonx.ai and AWS Titan models available through their bedrock services.

Defining Prompt Engineering

Prompt engineering is a recently evolved discipline. This discipline is going to help in design and develop best prompts to efficiently use the power of large language model and able to generate content. This discipline evolved with evolution of Large Language Model. For Large Language Model to provide correct and contextually relevant replies, prompt engineering is essential. It is Process or method for improving the output of large language models.

However, there are instances when Generative AI Tool like ChatGPT does not provide the correct output or precise response. You need to start applying Prompt engineering to address such problems. Prompt Engineering discipline guides us, how to ask the questions with unique set of instructions or guidelines that can enable such tooling (like ChatGPT) to better comprehend the task at hand and respond with best response.

The ability to engineer effective prompts has become an invaluable skill. A prompt is a spark, a gateway to creativity and thought experimentation. Prompt engineering can unleash creativity, encourage innovation, and uncover deep discoveries by creating thought-provoking prompts.

An appropriate balancing act between specificity and openness is required for prompt engineering. A prompt should be specific enough to provide emphasis and direction, along with that, there should be openness enough to allow for a variety of interpretations and surprising findings too. By making such balance, prompt engineers can help everyone thinking innovative and uncover potential unexplored area.

Let's explore ChatGPT with one prompt & content generated against the prompt.

> **Reference link for Drug Discovery**- https://www.drugdiscoverytrends.com/generative-ai-impact-drug-discovery

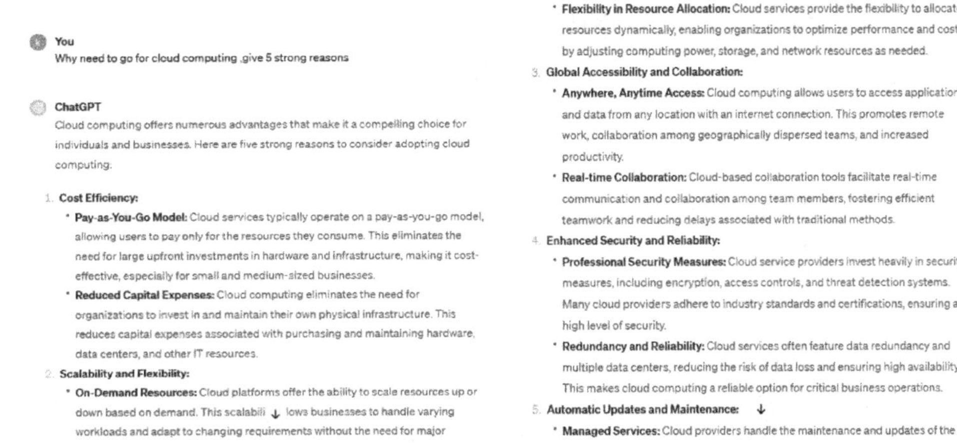

Figure 1.2: Prompting to ChatGPT

This discipline is getting used for extensive range of applications in various research topics, Innovations, and Industries too like Health care /Medicine, Banking, Insurance, Travel transportation, Retail, constructions /Mining's, Academics, drugs discovery so on.

In proceeding sections, we will discuss relevant examples to understand the prompt engineering:

Educations and learning

Traditional and Current educations are always oriented as passive and bookish knowledge. Consider curriculum material and timeline, Objective to complete the curriculum in required timeline and make students ready for exam. There was less room to think outside of the box. While faculty doesn't have much medium to address some out of the box or critical questions too. Now leveraging prompt engineering discipline, students and faculty can use the power of prompts/prompt engineering/Large Language model to have more innovative and critical brainstorming and exploration. This can give a new wing to education/Academics without any second thought.

This is going to uncover many what, why and how type of questions, which students are not able to get the answer as of today. Students are also very curious about many topics /knowledge. Students can explore these Generative AI along with Prompt engineering to gain a wide variety of knowledge which is easily accessible today.

Problem solving, Innovation and Research

Prompt engineering gives wings to problem solving, innovations and research areas.

Individuals can use prompt to ask your problems, and this could result in actionable insights. Prompt engineering is a dynamic tool, which is resulting in better decision-making, quicker research procedures, and enhanced adherence to constantly changing regulatory requirements.

Individuals can leverage prompt to extract specific and valuable information from a dozen documents as well. There is a concept called Retrieval Augmented Generation (RAG). Using Prompt engineering along with RAG concept, you can prompt /query information from documents as well.

In the Medicine or Drug discovery domain, where precision, accuracy, and insights are top consideration, Generative AI, prompt engineering, data generation, programmatic data labeling is gaining the ground, businesses considering using the technology to speed up drug discovery while not to comprise critical factors.

Finance and Banking

Financial Investment decisions - Prompt engineering has powered the AI driven tools for financial data analysis like market trends, organization performance etc. This allows us to make more informed decisions with respect to investment. Fraud detection and prevention - AI-driven algorithms can easily analyze transactional data, identify suspicious patterns, and detect potential fraud cases. Stitching prompt engineering with AI driven tools able to help the fraud detection and prevention mechanism.

Enhancing the capability of customer service with AI driven Chatbots – Banks are adopting the virtual agent /Chatbot for serving their customer on finance or banking queries rather than keeping more operational /manual staff. With the help of prompt engineering, these chatbots able t0 respond to a variety of consumer inquiries, from basic account inquiries to complex financial product explanations.

Each Industries are currently exploring the power of prompt engineering to get the best value out of it.

Prompt engineering requires technical and non- technical skills to work with this discipline.

- Technical Skills
    - Natural Language Processing (NLP)
    - Language of AI Large Language Models (LLM)
    - Language to communicate with AI Models (Coding Skills)
- Non- Technical Skills
    - Creativity (Power of Imaginations)
    - Lateral thinking
    - Curiosity
    - Brainstorming
    - Empathy
    - Communication
    - Breaking down the problem into smaller piece

In preceding section, we have gone through the aspects and various examples to understand the prompt engineering in conclusion we can say that prompt engineering aims to use well-crafted messages to influence user behavior or guide them toward specific actions, whether it's making a purchase, subscribing to a service, or engaging with content. These prompts are strategically designed to enhance the user experience and achieve desired outcomes.

Prompt Engineering / Large Language Model Use Cases

On a prominent level, Large Language Model supports various use cases. We need to think about how to get the best outcome around these use cases using prompt engineering.

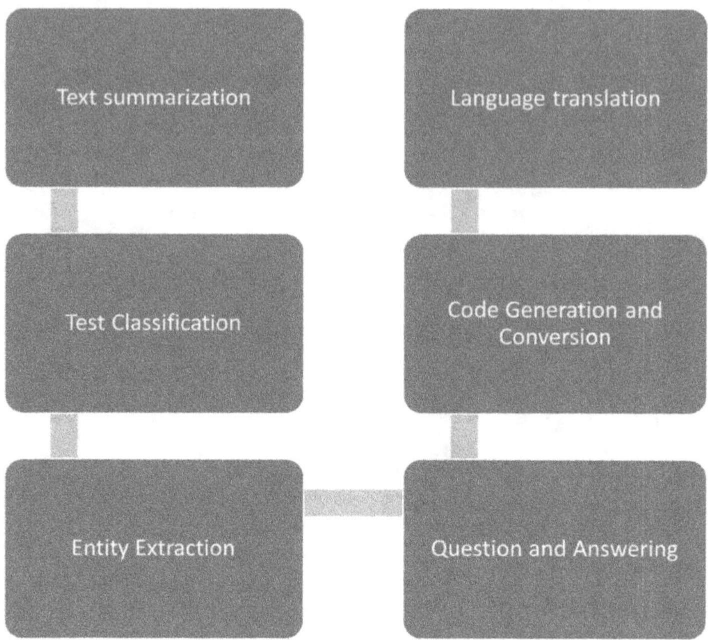

Figure 1.3: Visualizing LLM Use-cases

Text Generation

Generative AI Tool can generate new content for marketing, blogging and publishment or so. Please find below an example using ChatGPT.

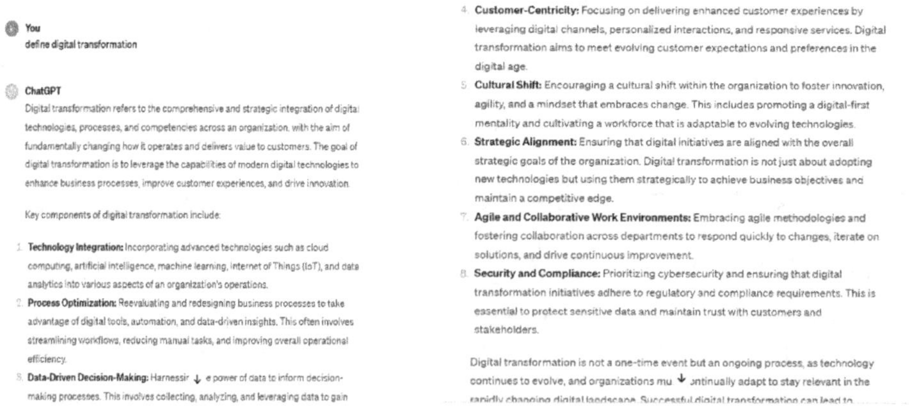

Figure 1.4: Text/Content Generation

You can try any topic for content generation/creation.

Text Summarization

Few Large Language Model are good and support the text summarizations as Flan-ul2-20b from Hugging face. Basically, the tool can help to summarize big email, documents content, meeting transcript for minutes of meeting (MOM) etc.

Figure 1.5 Minutes of Meeting- 1

Michael: How about the migration plan? Have we outlined the steps for transitioning to the new architecture?

David: We've created a detailed migration plan that includes phased migration of functionalities and thorough testing at each stage. Our goal is to minimize disruption to the business operations during the transition.

Emily: That sounds comprehensive. Do we have any specific challenges or risks that we need to address?

John: One concern I have is ensuring data integrity during the migration process. We need to make sure that all data is accurately transferred to the new systems without any loss or corruption.

Sarah: Agreed. We're implementing data validation checks and backup procedures to mitigate any potential risks.

Michael: How about the timeline for the modernization and migration work?

David: We're currently on track with our timelines. The modernization of the CRM system is scheduled to be completed by the end of next month, followed by the inventory management system in two months.

Emily: Let's make sure to keep communication channels open throughout the process and address any issues proactively.

John: Absolutely. If there are no further questions, I think we can conclude today's meeting. Thank you all for your updates and contributions.

Michael: Thanks, everyone. Have a great day.

Figure 1.6: Minutes of Meeting –2

ChatGPT

Discussion Highlights:

- Sarah provided updates on completing the analysis of legacy systems, targeting the CRM and inventory management platforms for modernization.
- The decision was made to adopt a microservices architecture for both systems to enhance scalability and efficiency.
- David outlined a detailed migration plan, aiming to minimize disruption to business operations through phased migration and thorough testing.
- Concerns were raised about ensuring data integrity during migration, addressed by implementing data validation checks and backup procedures.

Action Item:

- **Owner:** Sarah
- **Action:** Implement data validation checks and backup procedures to ensure data integrity during the migration process.

Message ChatGPT...

Figure 1.7: Minutes of Meeting –3

Text Classification

Text classification is a technique that **allocates** a set of predefined categories to open-ended text. One of the fundamental tasks in natural language processing is text classification. Examples of Text Classifications are sentimental analysis, intent detection, spam detection, automatic ticket routing and triaging.

Let's try with ChatGPT for Text Classification use case. ChatGPT is able to identify the Writers emotions very well.

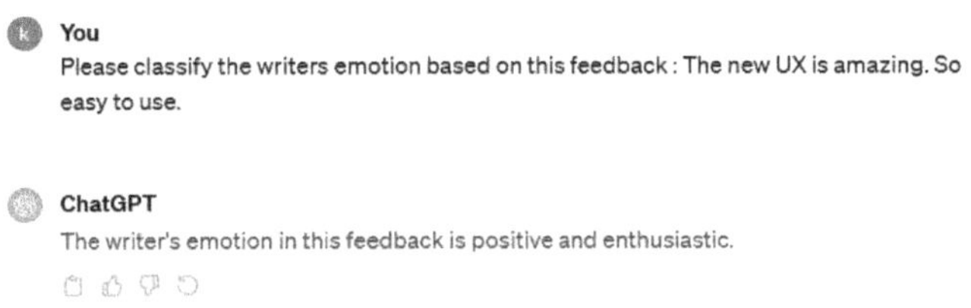

Figure 1.8: Text Classification Visualizing LLM Use-cases

Entity Extraction

Entity extraction is a text analysis technique. It automatically extracts a specified dataset from unstructured text using natural language processing (NLP) and categorizes it into predetermined groups.

Let's try ChatGPT on this use case. I prompted ChatGPT with instructions to extract the entities from provided text or content. It can successfully be extracted as below.

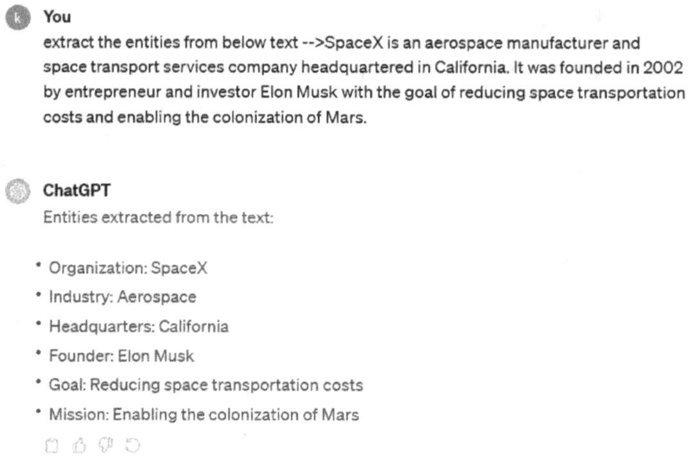

You

extract the entities from below text -->SpaceX is an aerospace manufacturer and space transport services company headquartered in California. It was founded in 2002 by entrepreneur and investor Elon Musk with the goal of reducing space transportation costs and enabling the colonization of Mars.

ChatGPT

Entities extracted from the text:

* Organization: SpaceX
* Industry: Aerospace
* Headquarters: California
* Founder: Elon Musk
* Goal: Reducing space transportation costs
* Mission: Enabling the colonization of Mars

Figure 1.9: Entity Extraction Example Visualizing LLM Use-cases

Questions and Answering

One of use case is Queston and Answer. If you have some information available, you want to respond to the questions only from the available information, if you find the answer, please respond and if you don't find the answer, say I don't know or as required. This is another, particularly good usecase. We can also try searching big documents too for this scenario. This can be powerful use case to solve many bigger problems.

Let's try ChatGPT on this use case.

You

Answer the following question using only information from the article. If there is no good answer in the article, say "I don't know".

Article:
###
Tomatoes are one of the most popular plants for vegetable gardens. Tip for success: If you select varieties that are resistant to disease and pests, growing tomatoes can be quite easy. For experienced gardeners looking for a challenge, there are endless heirloom and specialty varieties to cultivate. Tomato plants come in a range of sizes. There are varieties that stay very small, less than 12 inches, and grow well in a pot or hanging basket on a balcony or patio. Some grow into bushes that are a few feet high and wide, and can be grown is larger containers. Other varieties grow into huge bushes that are several feet wide and high in a planter or garden bed. Still other varieties grow as long vines, six feet or more, and love to climb trellises. Tomato plants do best in full sun. You need to water tomatoes deeply and often. Using mulch prevents soil-borne disease from splashing up onto the fruit when you water. Pruning suckers and even pinching the tips will encourage the plant to put all its energy into producing fruit.
--> What varieties of tomatoes are there?

ChatGPT

The article mentions that there are endless heirloom and specialty varieties of tomatoes to cultivate. It provides information about different sizes and growth habits of tomato plants, including small varieties for pots or hanging baskets, bush varieties, huge bush varieties, and long-vine varieties that love to climb trellises.

Figure 1.10: Information retrieval augmented generation example

IT – Code Generation or translation

In Information technology, Digital transformation and business transformation is on boom due to ever changing technology, evolving new and improved frameworks/languages and new trends additions like microservices, cloud computing, Data warehouse or Data Lake etc. During any customer business transformation/digital transformation journey or cloud adoption, they are looking forward to how quickly we can move or adopt new languages or modernize their system. For example, Code conversation from Cobol to opensource language, code explanations of complex and tedious old PLSQL code etc.

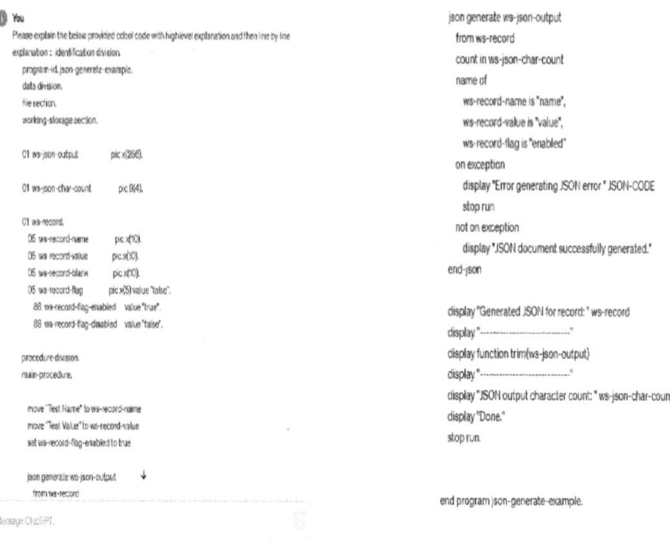

Figure 1.11: Cobol Code Explanation Example

ChatGPT

High-Level Explanation:

This COBOL code demonstrates the generation of JSON (JavaScript Object Notation) from COBOL data structures. It defines a COBOL program named `json-generate-example` which generates JSON output based on a defined COBOL record structure. The JSON output includes fields for `name`, `value`, and `enabled`, representing different attributes of a record.

The program first defines the necessary data structures in the `working-storage section`, including variables to hold the JSON output, character count, and a record structure. Then, in the `procedure division`, it sets values to the record fields, generates JSON from the record, handles exceptions if any, and displays the generated JSON output along with the character count.

Line-by-Line Explanation:

- `identification division.`: This division identifies the program.
- `program-id. json-generate-example.`: Specifies the program name.
- `data division.`: This division declares the data used by the program.
- `file section.`: It specifies files used by the program. (Not used in this code.)
- `working-storage section.`: It declares working storage variables.
  - `01 ws-json-output pic x(256).`: Defines a variable `ws-json-output` to hold the generated JSON output, with a maximum length of 256 characters.
  - `01 ws-json-char-count pic 9(4).`: Defines a variable `ws-json-char-count` to hold the character count of the JSON output.
- `01 ws-record.`: Defines a record structure `ws-record`.
  - `05 ws-record-name pic x(10).`: Field for the record name.
  - `05 ws-record-value pic x(10).`: Field for the record value.
  - `05 ws-record-blank pic x(10).`: Unused field.
  - `05 ws-record-flag pic x(5) value "false".`: Field for a record flag, initialized to "false".
    - `88 ws-record-flag-enabled value "true".`: Flag indicating if the record is enabled.
    - `88 ws-record-flag-disabled value "false".`: Flag indicating if the record is disabled.
- `procedure division.`: This division contains the actual processing logic of the program.
  - `main-procedure.`: Entry point of the main procedure.
  - `move "Test Name" to ws-record-name`: Assigns "Test Name" to the `ws-record-name` field.
  - `move "Test Value" to ws-record-value`: Assigns "Test Value" to the `ws-record-value` field.
  - `set ws-record-flag-enabled to true`: Sets the `ws-record-flag-enabled` flag to true.
  - `json generate ws-json-output ... end-json`: Generates JSON output from the `ws-record` structure, specifying the field names and their corresponding values.
  - `on exception ... not on exception ... end-json`: Handles exceptions during JSON generation, displaying error messages if any.
  - `display "Generated JSON for record: " ws-record ...`: Displays the generated JSON output along with other information.
  - `end program json-generate-example`: Marks the end of the program.

Figure 1.12: Cobol Code Explanation Example continuation of Figure 2.1

Language translation

This is a usecase, which can help to convert any language to any other language. From example from English to Dutch or Spanish to English or so.

Let's try ChatGPT!

Figure 1.13: Language translation example

Best Practices of Prompt engineering

There are a few best practices which need to be consider while working with Prompt Engineering.

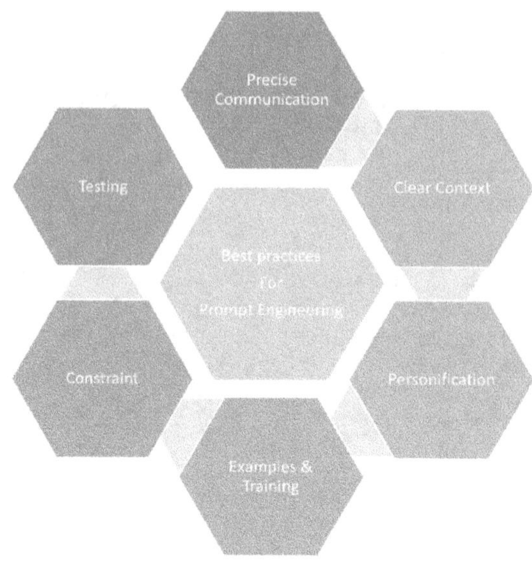

Figure 1.14: Visualizing Best Practices of prompt engineering.

Precise Communication

Creating precise and well-defined prompts to efficiently communicate the intended task or inquiry. When prompts are unclear, people may respond inadvertently or incorrectly.

Clear Context

Giving the model important background knowledge or context within the prompt will help in its understanding of the task. This technique can help to largely improve the response quality.

Personification

Providing the AI model, a personality or character to adopt when generating responses. This can be useful in creating a more engaging or relatable interaction. This is particularly useful when you want the model to perform a task or play a certain part in a conversation. These techniques are often employed in chatbots, virtual assistants, and role-playing scenarios to enhance the quality and context of the AI's responses.

Examples/Training

As we understand that large language Model supports various use cases as discussed above in section -Prompt Engineering / Large Language Model Use Cases

Each use case required a different type of training. For example,

- Include specific examples or demonstrations in the prompt to guide the model towards generating the desired output. This is valid in summarization or information extraction.
- While for text classification, you need to provide the example or training data for each classification.
- Some time, you need to train the model on specific dataset called. This is called as Fine tuning.

Constraint /Limitations

This is an especially important aspect to help the model narrow it focus and guide the model's behavior. For instance, you might instruct the model to answer a question without using a particular word or to keep responses concise or if model do not know the answer, it will return the response saying I don't know rather than giving inaccurate information.

Testing /Iteration

Another important aspect to continuously refine and testing prompts to achieve the desired outcome.

The Benefits of Creative Prompts

With Prompt Engineering, engineers just not be having only technical, they require various non-technical skills too i.e., creativity, curiosity, communication, dealing bigger problems to break into small once, empathy, feedback, Linguistics etc. Having these skills, engineers can leverage the full potential of creative prompt and Generative AI.

Engineers need to think creatively and beyond the box as prompts are no longer merely questions, but rather visionary catalysts. Creative prompts encourage the generative AI to provide original results and investigate unusual scenarios. As a result, being creative is not only essential for a prompt engineer, is a desired quality.

Creative prompting is motivation to ignite the creative thoughts to Unlocking Imagination, Adventurous Learning, solving problems in new ways, discovery of hidden treasures, finding valuable gems, Boost Innovation, Storytelling, Poem writing, discover artistic media, endless adventures.

Unlocking Imagination

Creative prompts can unlock the imagination and help to reveal many hidden ideas which were waiting to be discovered. This required engineers' creativity with prompts.

Enhance Learning

Users can keep enhancing their learning by asking questions in such a creative and sometime little open-ended way to explore the knowledge of these tooling and build the adventurous learning curve for themself. Anybody can have limitless learning with creative prompts.

Problem solving

Creative Prompting can help to solve complex problems too. Prompt engineers' tasks involve problem solving as well. Prompt engineering helps beginners to practice problem solving with the help of designing creative prompts.

Inspire Innovations & discover the hidden treasure!

Prompt engineers can discover innovative ideas by designing and probing with creative prompts. This led to generating new and innovative ideas but should be in the direction of human benefits only.

Story telling

Authors/Writers can leverage creative prompt and generative AI to generate new stories or poem altogether in new way. It is all about creativity of users.

For example - I am trying the ChatGPT with storytelling prompt. Here is my prompt.

Figure 1.15: Prompt to ChatGPT

Story telling Text generation by ChatGPT

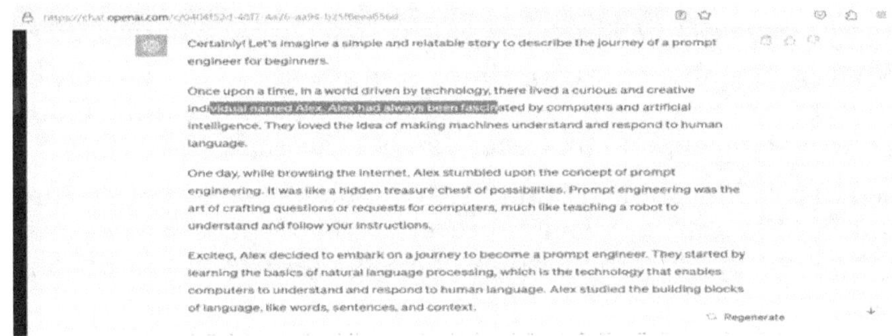

Figure 1.16: Text generated by ChatGPT against for Figure 2.5

Discovery of Artistic Media

Prompt engineering has huge scope in the art and media. With creative prompts, the author or artist can generate the new images, audio, or video. Creative prompt can overcome the authors blocks and can provide the new wings to their thoughts.

Personal Growth

Creative prompts can support personal growth and self-expression. This can lead to new thoughts, experiences which can lead to better personal development and self-awareness.

The Psychology of Prompts

Yes, Prompts are inquiring or questions in human language. There are psychological factors that influence how prompts are perceived, processed, and responded either by human intellectual or by AI Models. It is nothing but a cognitive process of AI Models, which process the prompts.

It is good to understand the human intellectual and their cognition & their psychological factors. These factors influence human cognition and equally map to the AI models cognition too.

Psychological principles of effective prompts are detailed out below.

Attention and Salience

The ability to purposefully focus on information while excluding unnecessary stimuli is a basic cognitive function, known as attention. It is equally important to consider the salience i.e., fact or importance of the information while creating effective prompt so that user can get the expected response.

Users need to consider some techniques to highlight the fact of the information like making bold or italic or visual representation of specific word or so as part of prompting so that AI model cognition system give attention on salience part.

Memory and Retrieval Cues

Memory is a fundamental principle of human cognition and AI models too. AI Models deeply trained on the huge data set to build their memory.

In human cognition as well as in prompt engineering, retrieval cues are techniques that help to retrieve the right response with the help of direct and simple question, having right context, using familiar phrases or patterns if possible.

In human conversations too, when two people interacted in the past. Later they connected after so long, they used to converse by providing some context of the past, what they had conversed etc. Retrieval cues are important factors to retrieve the right response from human cognition and AI models too.

Schema Activation and Knowledge Representation

The human brain has a concept of Schemas. When some scenarios or experiences happen with humans, this knowledge is arranged and stored using some pertinent schemas in the human cognition system.

When somebody tries to retrieve such information from human cognition then it is required by providing input questions /prompt in such a manner which can retrieve or activate the required schemas. This retrieval process is called schema activation.

There are some techniques for schema activation like providing context with background information, providing examples or scenarios which can lead to schema activation and AI models have clear understanding what task has been requested.

Motivation and Goal-oriented Behavior

It is important to develop motivating and interesting prompts. It is to incorporate users' interests or aspirations into the designing of effective prompts. If User is engaged with their personal interest or research on new topics or skills development, he or she can be more personally engaged and motivated. They can devote time and energy into this area and frame effective prompts towards getting more accurate and required outcomes using effective prompting and AI models.

Prompts can have elements of curiosity, challenge, originality when user are motivated and engaged for explorations and competence building exercise with this tooling.

Framing Effects and Cognitive Biases

Framing effects are the way, we present the prompt or question in such a way, which can lead to appropriate decision -making or judgments. But the user must be very clear, precise and avoid the ambiguity in the language so that there should not be any cognitive biases.

By carefully designing the effective prompts using appropriate words and phrases, this can minimize the biases and improve the accuracy of the AI model responses. To accomplish this, prompts should be written with the main components of the work in mind and should not include any unnecessary or misleading information.

By leveraging these principles like attention with fact, memory and retrievals cues, schemas activation, framing and motivation with effective designing of prompts , that can lead of more accurate and relevant responses back to users. This can help to provide more engaging user experience.

Conclusion

We have discussed Artificial Intelligence and their sub stream like Machine Learning, Deep Learning, Generative AI, Prompt Engineering and Large Language Model. We also covered detailing on prompt engineering along with their applicability in the various industries. We tried to touch base the various technical use cases for prompt engineering and along with non-technical aspects that needs to be considered with prompt engineering.

Along with that, we have covered the Psychology of Prompts, which includes various pointers like attention and salience, memory and retrieval clues, schema activation & knowledge representation, motivation and goal-oriented behavior and framing effects and cognitive basics.

In the next chapter, you will read various aspects related to Art and Science for crafting prompts.

Exercise: Test Your Understanding

Answer the following questions and test your understanding of learning from Chapter 1:

Q. 1. What is Prompt Engineering?

Q. 2. What are the use cases of Large Language model or prompt engineering?

Q. 3. What are the benefits of creative prompts?

Q. 4. What are the psychological principles of human cognition?

Do You Know?
Prompt Engineering is a technique that uses specific triggers to stimulate creative thinking, problem-solving, and innovation. It can be applied across various fields, from art and writing to business and education..

Chapter 2

The Art and Science of Crafting Prompts

The creation of a compelling prompt is a blend of art and science. It requires artistic qualities such as creativity, intuition, and a profound grasp of language, while also relying on scientific principles that are rooted in the mechanics of how AI models process request for information i.e. prompts and produce responses.

Initially crafting prompts was considered more of a technical task such as the focus was on getting a semantically accurate response. The field has now evolved to generate more human-like well-crafted responses.

We must understand that AI systems are not merely chatbots and rather depend on them to collate and fetch the acquired knowledge by creatively crafting our prompts.

In this chapter, we will discuss:
- Principles of Effective Prompts
- Anatomy of a Well-Crafted Prompt
- Balancing Open-Ended and Specific Prompts

Principles of Effective Prompts

Large language models are trained on vast volumes of data, and they are able to forecast the subsequent word based on the input. After extensive training, these models acquire the ability to grasp not just the grammar of human languages, but also the semantics and meaning of words, general knowledge, and fundamental logic.

Following certain principles of prompt engineering help to produce outputs as close to the desired outcome.

Principle 1: Write Clear Instructions

Giving clear instructions in the prompt is the most important principle of prompt engineering that can lead to the desired output.

This also involves having the clarity of thought in your mind to be able to articulate it well.

However, writing clear does not imply writing short instructions. Sometimes, longer prompts provide more clarity and context that will lead the model to produce a more accurate response.

An example of unclear prompt and response by ChatGPT:

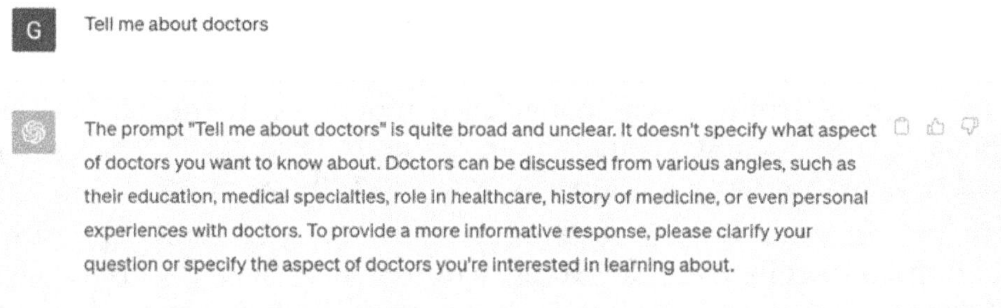

Figure 2.1: *Unclear Prompt example*

Refining the prompt from Figure 2.1:

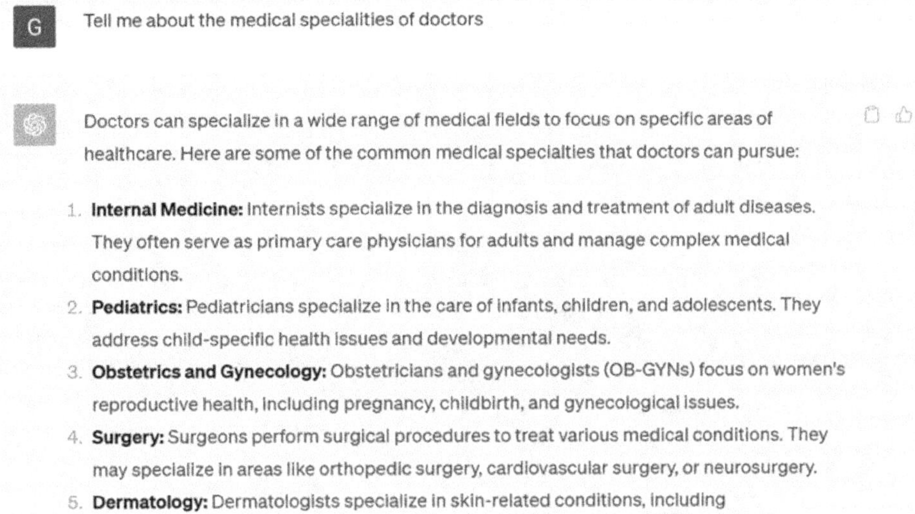

Figure 2.2: *Refined Prompt*

The above example shows how "Clarity" in the instruction affects the output
of the prompt.

Principle 2: Provide Context

The instruction in the prompt must also providing relevant background or
context to ensure the model understands the task or query.

The more detailed and specific the context, the model would understand it
better.

Example of no context prompt:

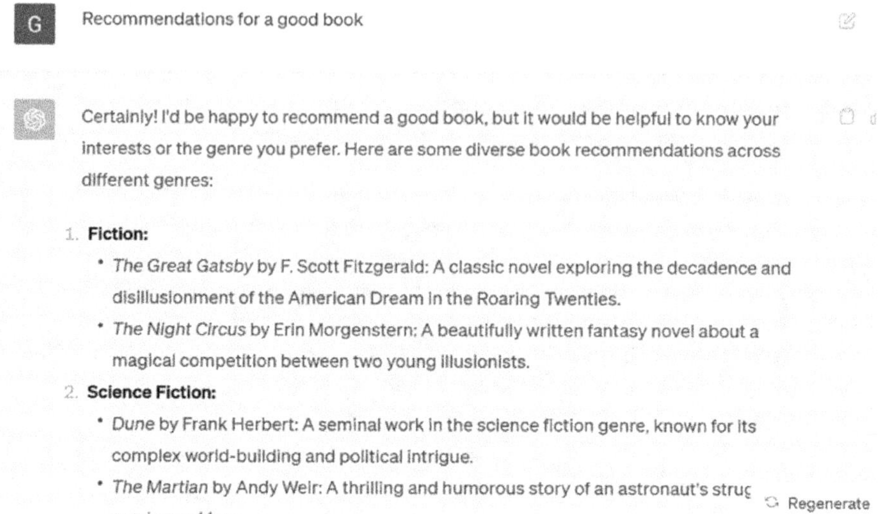

Figure 2.3: *No-context Prompt*

The above prompt does give recommendations, but the expected output needed maybe more specific like:

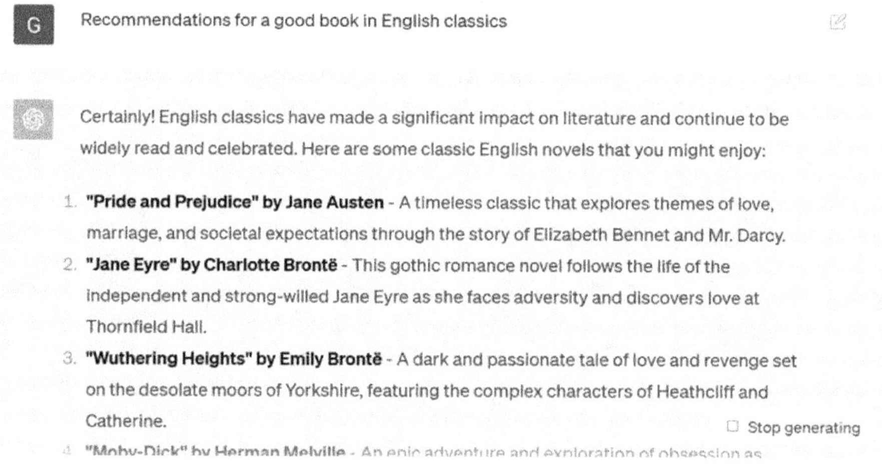

Figure 2.4: *Context Prompt*

Principle 3: Formatting the prompt

The format of a prompt is not definite as it depends on the goal we want to accomplish. The prompt thus should have clear instructions and the context of the problem.

General guiding principles that work better for an effective prompt are:

- Put instructions at the beginning of the prompt and use ### or """ to separate the instruction and context.
- Use commands such as "write," "summarize," and "translate." Experiment with several keywords to determine which produces the greatest results.
- Use one or more-line breaks to divide the instructions, examples, context, and input data.

You can try practicing with specific prompt structures:

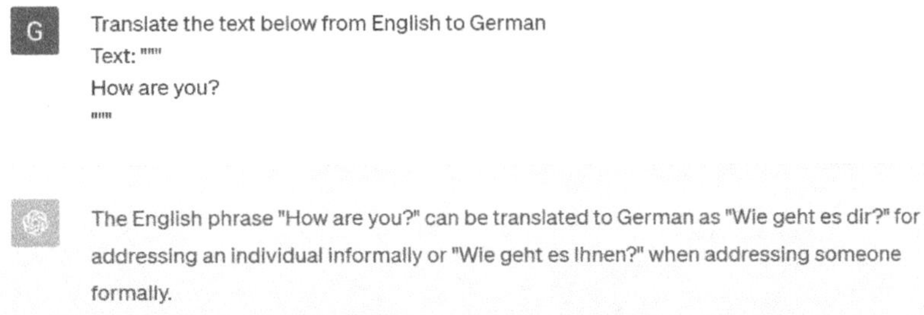

Figure 2.5: Example of a Prompt Structure

In the figure above, the example shows a simple prompt structure with a command and an input text.

Example: Below is another example of a prompt structure which begins with an instruction and command. It provides the input text and the output expected as a placeholder.

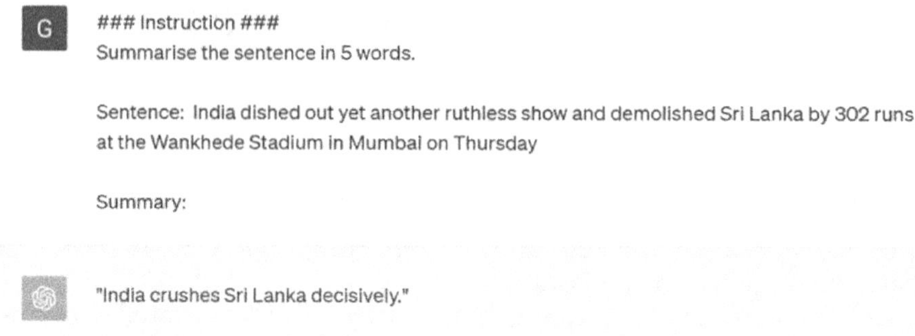

Figure 2.6: *Example of a Prompt Structure*

In the figure above, the example shows a simple prompt structure with an instruction, command and an input text.

Example: Below example shows how the model retains the context in the same session.

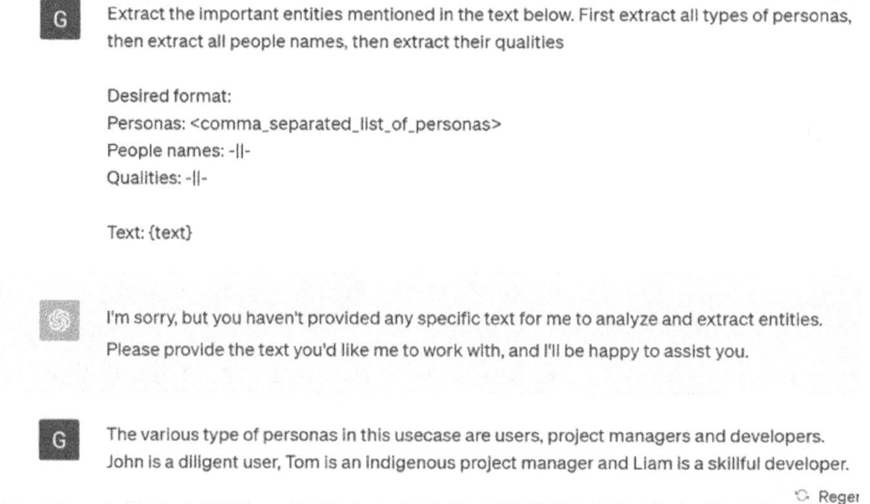

Figure 2.7: *Example showing the context in models*

Notice how in the above example, the model retains the context for the following text given in the next interactions.

Principle 4: Provide Examples

In this approach, the prompt includes examples of the desired output that guide the AI model to generate responses based on those examples.

It is useful when you want the model to learn from specific examples and mimic the desired behavior in terms of style, tone, or specific patterns.

Principle 4: Provide Balanced Prompts

Specifying precise information or guidance within a prompt enhances the precision of the generated response. When you define the context, parameters, or desired result, you assist the language model in creating responses that are closer to the desired response.

However, it's important to strike a balance, as overly specific prompts can constrain creativity and the scope of the generated content. Leaving some room for interpretation and open-ended exploration can foster more engaging and varied responses.

We will explore more on this balance in the following section.

Principle 5: Keep getting better

Prompt engineering gets better as we go through several iterations of refinement and observing the output generated. As the model gets mature, we also get to the point where we can give the appropriate instructions in accordance with the previously discussed principles. Thus, it is a continuous improvement process and our goal is to continually enhance the quality of our instructions.

Absolutely, it's quite common for two individuals to receive different responses from ChatGPT even when using the same prompt. Here are a few reasons why this might happen:

- Diversity in Model Versions: OpenAI frequently updates and refines the underlying model powering ChatGPT. As a result, different users might be interacting with slightly different versions of the model, leading to variations in responses.
- Contextual Understanding: ChatGPT generates responses based on the context provided in the prompt. Even slight variations or nuances in the way the prompt is formulated or presented can lead the model to generate different responses.
- Randomness and Probability: ChatGPT employs probabilistic methods to generate responses. It doesn't follow a deterministic pattern, so even if the

prompt is the same, the model might choose different responses probabilistically.

- Training Data and Previous Interactions: The model's responses might also be influenced by the vast and diverse training data it has been exposed to, as well as its previous interactions with users. This can result in different responses for different users.
- Model Size and Configuration: Depending on the deployment environment or API settings, different users might interact with models of varying sizes or configurations, leading to subtle differences in responses.

All these factors, among others, contribute to the variability in responses from ChatGPT. It's an inherent characteristic of AI models, and while they aim for consistency and coherence, some level of variation is expected due to the complexity and probabilistic nature of language generation.

Zero Shot Prompting Technique

As mentioned previously, LLMs are pre-trained models that understand the meaning of words and thus Zero shot prompting i.e. relying solely on an LLM's pre-trained information to answer a given user prompt.

Example of Zero shot Prompting

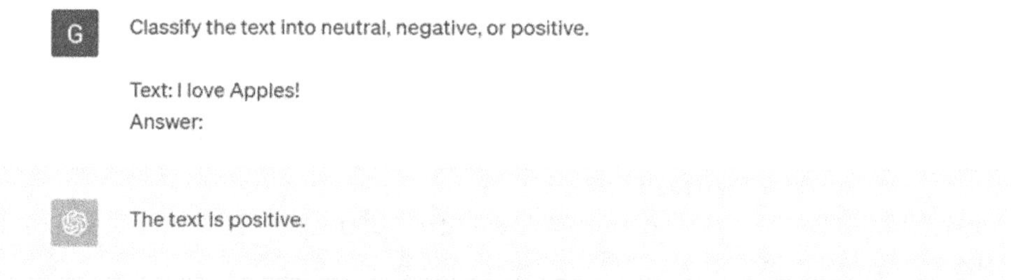

Figure 2.8: *Example of Zero-shot Prompting*

Above Example illustrates the Zero-Shot Prompting technique where the prompt instruction does not provide any examples.

Few Shots Prompting technique

To indicate the format or shape that you want the model response to be, we must include one or more pairs of examples input and corresponding desired output that helps the AI model to perform in-context learning to improve its performance.

Some tips to follow while providing examples:

- Use consistent formatting in the examples.
- Provide examples in random order. For example, mix the negative and positive up as the order might bias the model.
- Use labels.

Example of Few Shots Prompting

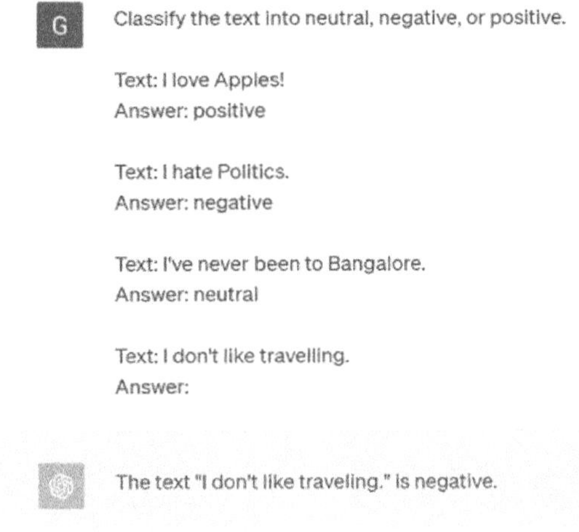

Figure 2.9: Example of Few-Shots Prompting

Above Example illustrates the Few-Shots Prompting technique where the prompt instruction provides few examples to the model.

More Tips and Tricks

Below are some tips and tricks that will help you craft an effective prompt.

- Prepare yourself to try new things and learn with each iteration of experimentation and refining your prompt.
- Begin with straightforward, zero-shot prompting technique and gradually increase their complexity until the necessary level of response accuracy is achieved. With every iteration of your question, you can expand on the context and examples. Try using another model if you're not noticing any

improvements.
- Prompts may include directives or queries for the model to answer. They might also include further details like context or background.
- Always use the newest models available.

Anatomy of a Well-Crafted Prompt

The following elements comprise the basic structure of prompts:

- Role: Giving AI a role to play during the conversation and telling what to do
- Instruction: The task that the model is given to accomplish
- Context: The model adapts to the problem more efficiently when it is in context.
- Input: It is the input provided to the prompt as a whole
- Action: Defining a clear and direct action to be taken with all the information
- Examples: Providing examples guides the model to generate desired output
- Output: Suggesting the desired output format

Using the above in a prompt lead to an almost complete prompt which may provide the right direction to the model to provide the expected output.

Example: The below example illustrates all elements of a prompt

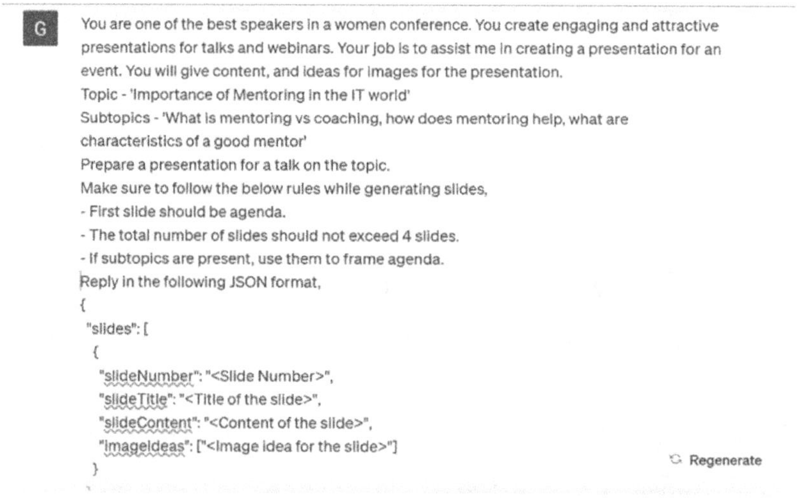

Figure 2.10: aExample showing Elements of a Prompt

Above Example illustrates embedding all elements of a prompt including Role, Instruction, Context, Input, Action, Examples and an Output Format.

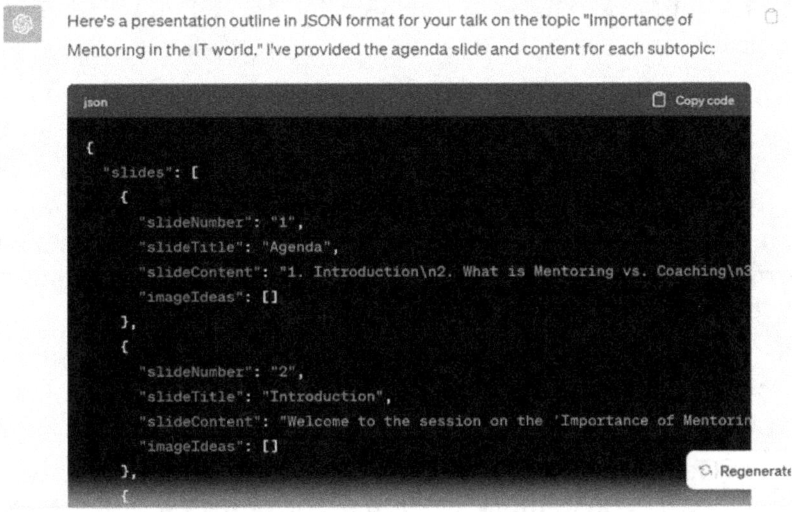

Figure 2.11: *Example response of the prompt in Figure 2.10*

Above example shows the output response from the prompt in `Figure 2.10` which illustrates a good output.

As seen in the above example, all elements of a prompt are covered, and the output is quite close to what we desired.

While such knowledge remains beneficial, what's more important is a thorough understanding and experience of how the AI responds to and interprets human language.

As said earlier, crafting a prompt is not a technical skill anymore and requires creativity and innovative thinking to get more out of the model.

Balancing Open Ended and Specific Prompts

An effective prompt is the one that achieves the clear goal the user wants. For that goal to be achieved, the prompt must have a balance between openness and specificity.

If prompts are too open-ended, they would not yield the desired goal and may get less/more information. It may also complicate the conversation with the chatbot.

Effective GPT prompts require a delicate balance between open-ended and specific questions. While open-ended prompts encourage users to provide more information, they can complicate the conversation and hinder the chatbot from achieving its intended goal.

Conversely, specific prompts can lead to quick resolutions but may narrow the conversation's scope. Achieving this balance is crucial in keeping users engaged while efficiently addressing their queries.

In the realm of Generative AI prompt engineering, crafting effective prompts is a skill. It demands a deep comprehension of the conversation's objectives, precise keyword and phrase selection, and the equilibrium between open-ended and specific prompts.

While specificity in a prompt can yield more precise responses, it is also important to leave prompts slightly open-ended. This flexibility enables the model to leverage its extensive training and offer insights or answers that may not be immediately apparent.

An example for an open-ended prompt may sound like "Tell me something interesting about the universe."

This would surely produce some interesting facts about the universe but may not give me what I desired.

On the other hand, if prompts are too specific, the conversation scope would become too limited, and the results might not be satisfactory.

An example of a very specific prompt could be:

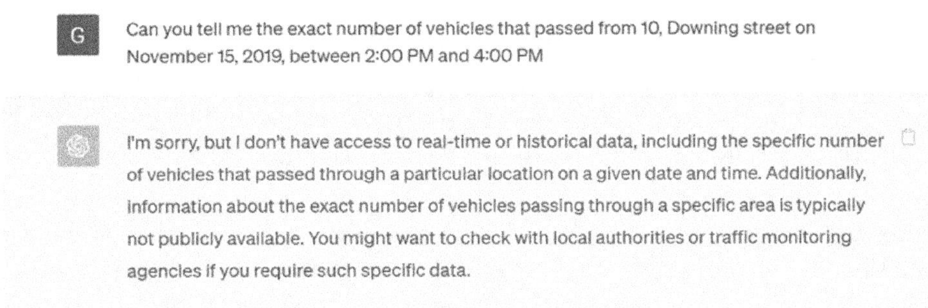

Figure 2.12: *Example of a very specific prompt*

As seen above, the chatbot should be thus encouraged to retrieve information from the expanse of knowledge that the model has acquired.

Therefore, finding a balance is the key to effective prompt engineering.

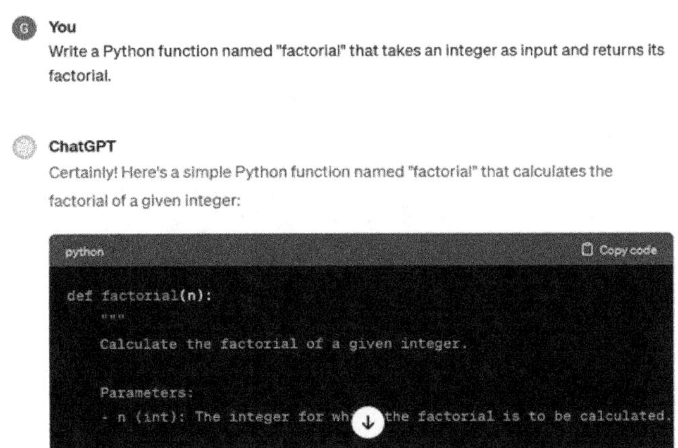

Figure 2.13: *Example of a Balanced Prompt*

In the above prompt, we see that the prompt instruction is balanced in terms of specificity, conciseness, clarity and open ended-ness yielding the expected output.

Framing effective prompts is an art that requires a deep understanding of the conversation goals, the right choice of keywords and phrases, and a balance between open-ended and specific prompts.

One important parameter that affects the generated output of the prompt is based on model creativity.

Most of the large language models have a 'temperature' configuration that talks about how creative or specific the responses can be. Also, in chat experiences like Microsoft Copilot on Edge browser allows the user to choose a conversation style that ranges from creative to balance too precise.

The value of temperature for ChatGPT ranges from 0 to 1. A value closer to 0 produces precise but less dynamic and more deterministic responses, while a value closer to 1 generates imaginative, diverse and creative responses.

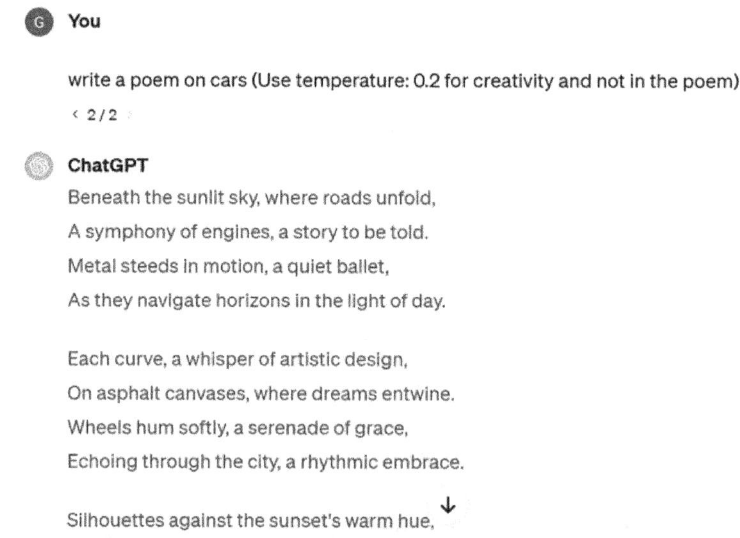

Figure 2.14: *Example of the "temperature" configuration in the prompt*

In the above examples, notice how the temperature value makes a difference in the output. The higher value of temperature generates a more diverse and creative poem.

Conclusion

In this chapter, we learnt basic and yet effective techniques to frame prompts that can unleash the knowledge from the AI models.

The next Chapter will explore how prompts can be used as catalysts for idea generation and brainstorming.

Exercise: Test Your Understanding

Answer the following questions and test your understanding of learning from Chapter 2:

Q. 1. What are the principles of effective prompts?

Q. 2. What is context in prompt engineering?

Q. 3. What is Zero Shot Prompting technique?

Q. 4. What is Few-Shots Prompting technique?

Q. 5. What does the "temperature" config determine?

Do You Know?
Effective prompts are clear, concise, and open-ended, encouraging multiple perspectives and solutions.

Chapter 3
Generating Ideas Through Prompts

This chapter will empower you with practical techniques to harness the power of prompts for idea generation and brainstorming. Whether you're a novice or have some experience in prompt engineering, these techniques will equip you to overcome mental barriers, expand on prompt-generated ideas, and generate creative concepts. By the end, you'll feel confident in your ability to apply these strategies effectively.

In this chapter, we will discuss:

- Prompt-Driven Idea Generation Techniques
- Overcoming Mental Barriers with Prompts
- Expanding on Prompt-Generated Ideas

Prompt-Driven Idea Generation Techniques

Idea generation, often called brainstorming, is the creative process of developing new and innovative concepts, solutions, or approaches. It involves thinking freely and exploring various possibilities without immediate judgment or criticism. This process is crucial in multiple fields, including business, science, education, and the arts, as it empowers individuals to find novel solutions to problems, fostering creativity along the way.

The Process of Idea Generation

If we take it in a typical scenario, don't think from a technical perspective; the idea can evolve with or without following any process.

Idea generation is the cornerstone of creativity and innovation, forming the basis for problem-solving and developing new concepts, products, and solutions. Whether you're an entrepreneur looking to start a new business, a writer seeking inspiration for your next novel, or an engineer tasked with designing cutting-edge technology, the ability to generate ideas is crucial.

At its heart, idea generation is a journey of liberation, a voyage into uncharted territories of thought, and a quest for possibilities beyond the realm of feasibility or practicality. This process liberates your creativity and encourages divergent thinking, allowing you to tap into your imagination and unearth unique insights. By fostering an environment where all ideas are embraced and explored, you create fertile ground for the seeds of innovation to blossom.

This section will explore the structured steps involved in idea generation. Each step is vital in nurturing creativity and transforming raw thoughts into viable concepts, from preparation and incubation to brainstorming, evaluation, and selection. We will also discuss various techniques and tools that can facilitate this process, providing you with practical strategies to harness your creative potential.

The general overall process of idea generation can be like that detailed below and visualized in `Figure 3.1`

Figure 3.1: Visualization of the process of Idea Generation

The process of Idea generation from the preceding image can evolve as below:

- **Preparation**: Understand the problem or objective clearly. Gather relevant information and resources to provide context.

- **Incubation**: This is a necessary step for your ideas to mature. Allow time for subconscious processing. This might involve taking breaks or engaging in unrelated activities. Trust in the power of your mind to work on the problem even when you're not consciously thinking about it.
- **Brainstorming**: This is your opportunity to let your creativity soar. Engage in activities stimulating free-thinking, such as group discussions, mind mapping, or solo ideation sessions. Feel the freedom to explore unconventional ideas.
- **Evaluation**: Assess the generated ideas based on feasibility, impact, and goal alignment.
- **Selection**: Choose the best ideas for further development and implementation.

Mastering the process of idea generation is not just about birthing good ideas; it's about nurturing a mindset that is open to new possibilities and resilient in the face of challenges. It's a journey of personal growth and empowerment. By the end of this exploration, you will be armed with the knowledge and techniques to birth a multitude of ideas, refine them, and breathe life into your most promising concepts, fueling your inspiration and motivation.

Techniques for Idea Generation

Generating innovative ideas is fundamental to creativity, problem-solving, and innovation. Whether you're a student, an entrepreneur, a scientist, or an artist, the ability to think creatively and develop new concepts can significantly impact your success and effectiveness. The idea generation process can often feel daunting, especially when faced with a blank page or a challenging problem. However, with the proper techniques, you can unlock your creative potential and consistently produce many ideas, reassuring you that your time invested in learning these techniques is valuable.

This section will introduce you to various techniques designed to stimulate your thinking, break through mental barriers, and empower you to generate many creative ideas. These versatile methods can be applied in multiple contexts, from individual brainstorming sessions to collaborative group efforts. By incorporating these techniques into your creative toolkit, you'll be better equipped to tackle complex problems, innovate within your field, and bring your ideas to life, fostering a sense of confidence in your creative abilities.

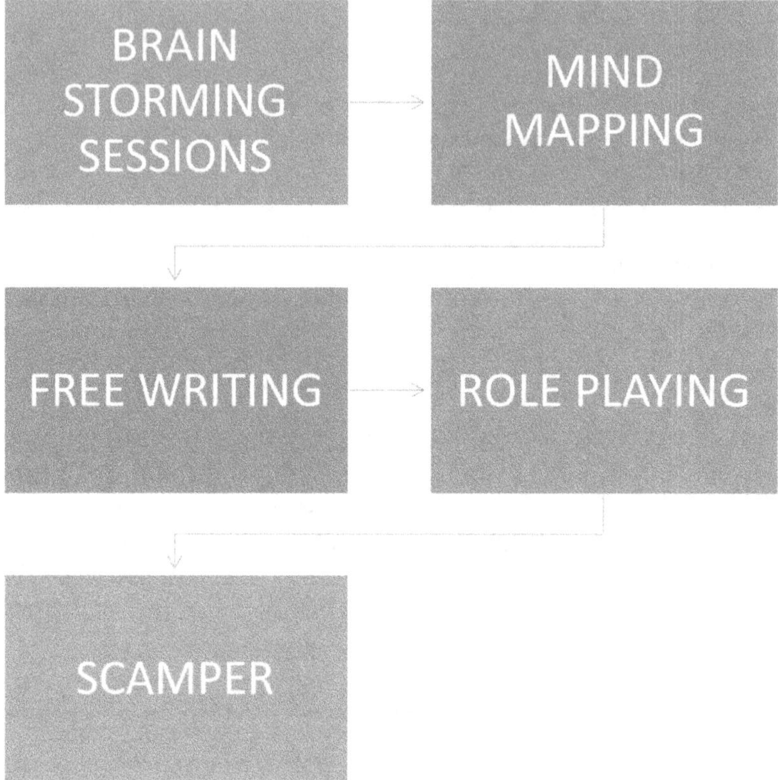

Figure 3.2: Visualization techniques for Idea Generation

We will explore traditional and modern approaches, from classic brainstorming and mind mapping to the more structured SCAMPER method and using prompts to guide your thinking. Each technique offers unique advantages and can be adapted to suit your specific needs and objectives, giving you the flexibility to apply them in various scenarios. Whether you're looking to generate ideas for a new product, solve a complex problem, or enhance your creative thinking skills, these techniques will provide the tools you need to succeed.

As depicted in `Figure 3.2`, these are the practical techniques we will be exploring. Each of these techniques is designed to enhance your creativity and innovation:

- **Brainstorming Sessions**: These are collaborative group or individual sessions where ideas are freely shared without judgment, fostering a sense of teamwork and shared creativity.
- **Mind Mapping**: A visual tool that organizes thoughts and evolves ideas' connections. It involves creating a central concept and branching out with

related subtopics, allowing for a clear and structured representation of complex information, which helps in brainstorming, planning, and problem-solving.
- **Free Writing**: This technique encourages you to write continuously for a set period, allowing your spontaneous thoughts to flow freely and without constraint, fostering a sense of liberation and openness to new ideas.
- **Role Playing**: Adopting different perspectives to explore new ideas.
- **SCAMPER**: A structured technique to stimulate creative thinking and innovation by guiding individuals through a series of questions to modify and transform existing ideas into new ones. The acronym stands for Substitute, Combine, Adapt, Modify, Put to another use, Eliminate, and Reverse. Each element prompts a different approach to reimagining ideas, products, or processes.

Refer to `Figure 3.3` that visualizes `SCAMPER`:

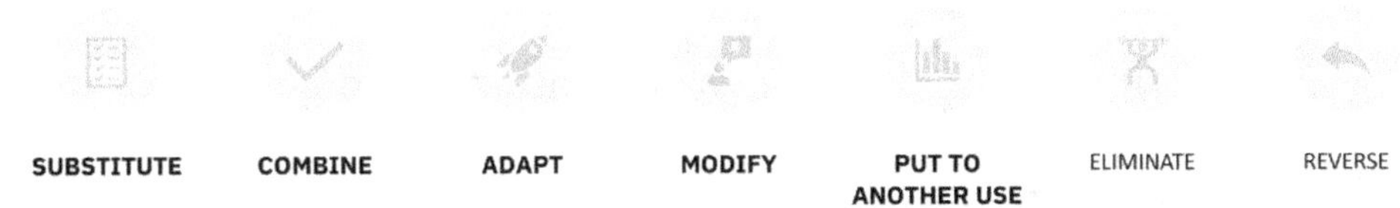

Figure 3.3: Visualization SCAMPER

Here's a detailed explanation of each component:
- **Substitute**: Consider replacing elements, materials, or processes with alternatives and, for example, substituting traditional printing methods with digital ones in publishing.
- **Combine**: Look for opportunities to merge ideas, features, or concepts. For instance, combining a book with an audiobook can create a new product that caters to different preferences.
- **Adapt**: Modify existing ideas to suit new conditions or needs. An example is adapting a traditional bookstore to include a coffee shop to attract more customers.
- **Modify**: Alter existing elements to improve or enhance them. For example, turning a traditional book into an interactive e-book with multimedia features can make reading more engaging.
- **Put to another use**: Explore new applications or markets for existing ideas. For instance, repurposing old books into art or furniture can create unique products.
- **Eliminate**: Identify and remove unnecessary or redundant elements.

Eliminating non-essential features from a product can streamline its design and reduce costs.

- **Reverse**: Consider reversing the order of operations or processes. Starting a book from the end can offer a fresh perspective, reversing the typical reading experience.

INFO: SCAMPER can be applied to various business aspects, such as product development, marketing strategies, and process improvement, to generate innovative ideas and solutions.

With prompt-driven idea generation, you have the freedom to use specific cues or stimuli, known as prompts, to stimulate your creative thinking and generate new ideas. These prompts can be questions, images, scenarios, phrases, or any other stimulus that sparks your imagination and inspires your creativity. This method provides a flexible structure that guides and focuses your ideation process, allowing you to explore and create without limitations.

Followings are the Prompt-driven idea generation techniques:

The Basics of Prompt-Driven Ideation

Prompts are not just cues or stimuli, they are the keys that unlock your imagination and inspire boundless creativity. They can take the form of questions, images, phrases, or scenarios, offering you a world of possibilities. The beauty of using prompts is that they invite you to approach them with an open mind, free from the constraints of conventional thinking, and a willingness to explore diverse perspectives.

Let's say you are part of a team tasked with designing a new type of smartphone. A simple prompt like, "What if smartphones were made entirely from biodegradable materials?" can spark a flurry of innovative ideas regarding sustainability, functionality, and design.

Divergent Thinking with Prompts

Divergent thinking is not just a method, it's a gateway to a world of creative possibilities. It's about exploring the unexplored, pushing the boundaries of what's possible. When using prompts, divergent thinking is about unleashing your ideas, brainstorming as many as you can, without worrying about their feasibility initially. This is where innovation begins.

Technique: Start with a broad prompt, such as "How can technology improve daily life?" Write down every idea that comes to mind, whether wild or impractical. This method helps you break free from conventional thinking patterns.

Mind Mapping

Mind mapping is not just a tool, it's a superpower that allows you to structure information and see connections between different ideas. It's like having a map of your thoughts, guiding you through the exploration of a prompt. Start with a central prompt and branch out with related ideas. This technique not only organizes your thoughts but also empowers you to take control of your creative process, encouraging a more profound exploration of the prompt.

Example: Using the prompt "`Future of education`," you might explore topics like online learning, virtual reality classrooms, personalized education, and gamification.

SCAMPER Technique

SCAMPER is an acronym for Substitute, Combine, Adapt, Modify, Put to another use, Eliminate, and Reverse. This technique involves asking questions related to each component to explore new possibilities.

Example: For improving a coffee maker, you might ask:

- **Substitute**: What if we substitute the heating element with solar power?
- **Combine**: Can we combine it with a grinder for fresh coffee?
- **Adapt**: How can we adapt it to work in a car?
- **Modify**: What if it had a timer to start brewing before you wake up?
- **Put to another use**: Can it also boil water for tea?
- **Eliminate**: What if we eliminate the need for disposable filters?
- **Reverse**: How about a coffee maker that cools the coffee instead?

While general idea generation relies on open-ended thinking and exploration, prompt-driven idea generation uses specific stimuli to guide and focus the creative process. Both methods have their strengths and can be used effectively depending on the context and objectives of the ideation process. By understanding the differences and benefits of each approach, you can choose the most suitable method to generate innovative and impactful ideas.

Overcoming Mental Barriers with Prompts

Writing prompts, or mental cues, are transformative tools that help individuals address and move past mental blocks or obstacles. These prompts, in the form of questions, statements, or exercises, are designed to stimulate thinking and encourage introspection. By engaging with these prompts, individuals can transform their thoughts and feelings, gaining new perspectives, and challenging limiting beliefs. This process is a catalyst for creativity, problem-solving, and personal growth. Ultimately, the goal is to help individuals transform their mental barriers, developing greater self-awareness, and a deeper understanding of themselves and their challenges.

Recognizing Mental Barriers

Mental barriers can significantly hinder creativity. These include fear of failure, perfectionism, and a fixed mindset. Recognizing these barriers is the first step towards overcoming them.

Example: If you're afraid of failing, remember that brainstorming is about generating ideas, not finding the perfect solution immediately.

Recognizing mental barriers is crucial for personal growth and development. Let's expand on the example:

Identifying the Barrier: In this example, the mental barrier is the fear of failing, which can inhibit creativity and problem-solving.

Explanation: The example suggests a profound shift in mindset by reframing the purpose of brainstorming. Instead of viewing it as a final search for a perfect solution, it encourages seeing it as a process of idea generation. This shift can help overcome the fear of failure by emphasizing that mistakes and imperfect ideas are natural and expected in the brainstorming phase.

Application: Individuals can approach brainstorming sessions with a more open and creative mindset by recognizing and understanding this mental barrier. They can focus on generating a wide range of ideas without the pressure of immediate perfection, leading to more innovative and effective solutions.

Impact: Overcoming the fear of failure in brainstorming can lead to a transformation in creativity, collaboration, and problem-solving skills. It can also help individuals become more resilient in the face of challenges, as they learn to see failure as a steppingstone to success rather than a setback.

Using Prompts to Break Through

Prompts can help bypass mental barriers by providing a structured starting point. They can redirect your focus from the obstacles to the possibilities.

Technique: If you're stuck, try using a disruptive prompt. For instance, "What would a child suggest?" This can help you think outside the box and break free from adult constraints.

Embracing disruptive prompts, such as 'What would a child suggest?', is a powerful strategy for overcoming mental blocks and rigid thinking patterns. When you find yourself grappling with a problem or feeling confined by conventional adult perspectives, this approach can open the door to a more imaginative and unrestricted mindset, leading to innovative solutions.

Children possess a unique problem-solving approach characterized by curiosity, openness, and a willingness to explore unconventional ideas. By adopting this perspective, you can challenge your assumptions, question established norms, and consider solutions that might not have occurred to you otherwise, fostering a more innovative mindset.

This technique is a catalyst for creativity and innovation. It liberates you from conventional thinking, encouraging fresh, innovative approaches to your challenges. By embracing a childlike sense of wonder and possibility, you can unlock new ideas and perspectives that can lead to breakthrough solutions, fostering a more innovative and creative mindset.

Embracing Imperfection

Prompts encourage exploration and experimentation. Accept that only some ideas will be a winner. The goal is to generate a broad range of ideas from which you can refine and develop the best ones.

Exercise: Set a timer for 10 minutes and write down as many ideas as possible for a given prompt. Please don't stop evaluating or judging them. This exercise can reduce the pressure to be perfect and encourage free-flowing creativity.

This exercise is designed to help individuals embrace imperfection and foster creativity by encouraging them to generate ideas without judgment or evaluation. Setting a timer for 10 minutes creates a sense of urgency, prompting participants to focus on quantity rather than quality of ideas.

The critical aspect of this exercise is to write down as many ideas as possible within the time limit without stopping to evaluate or judge them. This approach removes the pressure to develop perfect ideas and promotes a free-flowing stream of creativity. Allowing ideas to flow without restriction will enable participants to explore unconventional or unexpected ideas they might otherwise dismiss.

After the 10 minutes, participants can review their ideas and reflect on the process. They may discover that some initial ideas, which they might have considered imperfect or impractical, could be developed into innovative solutions or creative concepts. This exercise can help individuals overcome perfectionism and fear of failure, allowing them to embrace imperfection as a natural part of the creative process.

Expanding on Prompt-Generated Ideas

Expanding on prompt-generated ideas is a creative process that involves exploring, refining, and developing initial concepts into more detailed and fleshed-out narratives or projects. It's a process that harnesses the power of your imagination, requiring critical thinking and a deep understanding of the original prompt's themes or concepts. One approach is brainstorming additional details, such as character backgrounds, plot twists, or setting descriptions, that build upon the initial idea. Another method is considering different perspectives or angles from which the prompt can be approached, adding complexity and depth to the narrative. Through this process, writers can transform simple prompts into rich and engaging stories, essays, or creative works that captivate audiences and explore complex themes.

Deepening the Initial Idea

Once you have a pool of ideas, it's time to expand on them. Take one idea and explore it in depth. Ask questions like "Why?" "How?" and "What if?" to push the boundaries of the initial concept.

Example: If your prompt-generated idea is a solar-powered smartphone, ask:

- Why is solar power beneficial for smartphones?
- How can solar panels be integrated without affecting the design?
- What if the phone could also store excess energy for other devices?

Explanation

In the preceding example, we took a few points lets dive into details to understand the example:

Deepening the Initial Idea involves exploring various aspects and implications of a concept to develop it further. In the example of a solar-powered smartphone, this process would entail asking probing questions to enhance the idea's depth and potential:

- **Why is solar power beneficial for smartphones?**
  This question explores the advantages and value proposition of integrating solar power into smartphones. It could lead to discussions on environmental impact, sustainability, and user convenience.
- **How can solar panels be integrated without affecting the design?**
  This question addresses a crucial aspect of product development, focusing on the feasibility and aesthetics of incorporating solar panels into a smartphone's design. It could lead to innovative design solutions or material choices.
- **What if the phone could also store excess energy for other devices?**
  This question expands the idea by considering additional features and functionalities. It opens possibilities for creating a more versatile and useful product, potentially appealing to a wider range of consumers.

By asking these questions, you delve deeper into the initial idea, uncovering new perspectives and potential enhancements that can enrich the concept and make it more compelling.

Combining Ideas

Sometimes, the best ideas come from combining two or more concepts. Look for connections between ideas generated from prompts and see how they can be integrated.

Exercise: Take two unrelated ideas from your brainstorming session and find a way to merge them. For example, combining "virtual reality classrooms" with "gamification" could create immersive, game-based learning environments.

In the exercise `'Combining Ideas,'` the goal is to merge two unrelated ideas to create a new, innovative concept. This process often leads to unique and creative solutions, challenging you to think outside the box and empowering you to create something truly original.

For instance, let's consider two unrelated ideas: 'smartphone apps for mental health' and 'online fitness challenges.' By combining these, we could create a new concept, such as 'an app that tracks your mental health progress through online fitness challenges.' This innovative idea could potentially revolutionize the way we approach our well-being, allowing users to set fitness goals and track their mental well-being simultaneously, integrating physical and psychological health improvement.

Prototyping and Testing

After expanding on your ideas, create simple prototypes or mock-ups to test their feasibility. This doesn't have to be a physical model; it can be a sketch, a storyboard, or a digital simulation.

Example: If your idea is a new app, create wireframes or a clickable prototype to visualize the user experience. Gather feedback from potential users to refine your idea further.

Explanation

In the preceding example, we made a few points. This example illustrates the process of prototyping and testing in the context of developing a new app idea. Here's a breakdown:

- **Creating Wireframes or Clickable Prototype**: Before fully developing the app, it is beneficial to create a visual representation of its interface and functionality. Wireframes are simple, static layouts that show the basic structure of the app. Clickable prototypes, on the other hand, are more interactive and allow users to navigate through the app as if it were already developed.
- **Visualizing User Experience**: Wireframes and clickable prototypes help you visualize how users will interact with your app. This visualization is crucial for understanding the app's flow, identifying potential usability issues, and refining the user interface.
- **Gathering Feedback**: Once you have a prototype, you can gather feedback from potential users. This feedback can help you understand what users like and dislike about the app, what features are intuitive or confusing, and what improvements can be made.
- **Refining Your Idea**: Based on the feedback you receive; you can refine your app idea further. This might involve changing the user interface, adding or removing features, or adjusting the overall concept of the app.

Overall, prototyping and testing are essential steps in the app development process, as they help validate ideas, identify potential issues early on, and create a better user experience.

Iterative Development

Creativity is an iterative process. Use feedback from your prototypes to improve and evolve your ideas. Feel free to return to the drawing board and tweak your concepts based on new insights.

Technique: Keep a journal of your idea development process. Document the changes you make, the feedback you receive, and the emerging ideas. This helps track progress and ensure continuous improvement.

In the context of iterative development, keeping a journal of your idea development process is a valuable technique for several reasons:

- **Documenting Changes**: By recording the changes you make to your project, you create a historical record of its evolution. This can be invaluable for understanding why certain decisions were made and how the project progressed.
- **Tracking Progress**: A journal helps you track your progress toward your goals. Reviewing your journal regularly lets you see how far you've come and identify areas where you may need to adjust your approach.
- **Receiving Feedback**: Recording your feedback lets you capture different perspectives on your project. This can help you make informed decisions about how to improve it.
- **Emerging Ideas**: Sometimes, new ideas or insights emerge during development. By documenting these ideas, you can ensure they are remembered and can be explored further.
- **Continuous Improvement**: Documenting your idea development process creates a foundation for continuous improvement. You can review your journal regularly to identify areas for improvement.

Overall, keeping a journal of your idea development process is valuable for ensuring that your project continues to evolve and improve over time.

Conclusion

In this chapter, we learnt Prompts are powerful tools for generating creative ideas and overcoming mental barriers. Using techniques like divergent thinking, mind mapping, SCAMPER, and iterative development, you can harness the prompts' full potential to spark innovation and creativity. We also learnt that the goal should not to find a perfect idea immediately but to explore a wide range of possibilities and refine them over time..

In the next chapter, we will explore strategies for overcoming creative blocks and reigniting the spark of creativity using prompts. It provides detailed strategies and techniques for using prompts to break through artistic and mental barriers.

Exercise: Test Your Understanding

Answer the following questions and test your understanding of learning from Chapter 3:

Q. 1. What is divergent thinking, and how can it be applied using prompts?

Q. 2. Explain the SCAMPER technique and provide an example of its use.

Q. 3. How can prompts help in overcoming mental barriers to creativity?

Q. 4. Describe the process of expanding on a prompt-generated idea.

Q. 5. Why is it essential to embrace imperfection during the idea-generation process?

Chapter 4

Overcoming Creative Blocks with Prompt

In the last chapter, we have talked about the Prompt-Driven Idea Generation Techniques, Overcoming Mental barriers with Prompt and Prompt generated Ideas expansion Techniques.

Objective of this chapter to understand, what are creative blocks, Identifying the reasons of such creative blocks and possible techniques & strategies to overcome such creative blocks of the users. Certain period when users are not able to produce creative ideas/thinking. This problem can occur with users, working with different industries like academics, research, blogging, writing / authoring, content generation or what else.

We want to talk about the various techniques & strategies to overcome the creative blocks. Apart from Traditional, there are AI tools and Prompt techniques that can be useful to overcome the creative blocks and reignite the spark of creativity and navigate the users further.

In this chapter we will cover the below topics:
- Identifying and Understanding Creative Blocks
- The Conventional Method: Overcoming Writer's Block
- AI Method: Prompt Techniques for Overcoming Creative Blocks
- Navigating Through Artist's Block

Identifying and Understanding Creative Blocks

You're probably familiar with the condition known as writer's block, whether you're an experienced writer or a beginner attempting to find your voice. It can be really depressing to stare at a blank page with the cursor blinking back at you like a timer counting down the seconds.

When someone is creatively blocked, they don't have access to their creative impulses or modes of thinking. It's common for people in creative professions to face creative blocks periodically.

Creativity is one of the most important abilities for handling issues or solving problems in business.

Let's learn about some of the most frequent reasons for creative blocks if you find it difficult to think creatively or if your team finds it difficult to solve challenges creatively.

Anyone can experience a creative block, and it can happen for numerous reasons. Let's look at some of the most common causes for creative blocks.

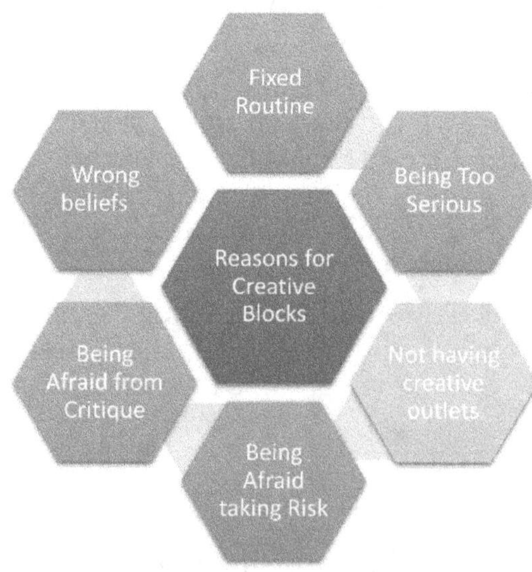

Figure 4.1: Reasons for creative Blocks

The preceding Image (Figure 4.1) dictates the Reasons for Creative Blocks. All the surroundings' hexagons are the common reasons for creativity block.

Let's understand each one of them in detail below.

Fixed Routine

Maintaining a healthy lifestyle and a productive work life both depend on having the appropriate routines and habits. On the other hand, a person's ability to think and express themselves creatively can be constrained by an overly rigid schedule.

- **Being Too Serious**: Some members of your team may be incredibly creative when it comes to their hobbies and personal lives, but they may find it difficult to think creatively at work. In the workplace, there is undoubtedly a focus on uniformity, conformity, and professionalism, which some people may find incompatible with their creative expression.

    Lack of Creative Outlets: If your surroundings don't seem to be encouraging creative thinking, it might be because none of the members of your team have any creative outlets in their personal or professional lives.

- **Being Afraid of Taking Risk**: Creativity can be severely hampered if you or your group are frightened of making mistakes, taking chances, or being incorrect. Being unwilling to commit even the smallest mistake can entirely derail creativity.

- **Being Afraid from Critique**: If you believe that your team's lack of creativity stems from their fear of having their ideas quickly shot down, try organizing brainstorming sessions that prioritize idea generation and collection followed by a second session dedicated to idea analysis and redlining.

- **Wrong Beliefs**: Some people may also think or associate creativity with certain professions versus others. Example Music, Dance, Painting, cooking, Marketing may be considered more creative professions compared to IT Services, Supply chain, Banking etc.

Now we understand the various reasons for creative blocks. Let's move forward to explore the solution to overcome these creative blocks.

The Conventional Method: Overcoming Creative Block

Traditionally, a variety of strategies can be used to get beyond creative blocks. Recall that getting past creative block is an individual and incremental process. Treat yourself with kindness, welcome trying new things, and let the creative juices flow again organically.

Here are some approaches to help users overcome creative blocks.

Figure 4.2: *Strategies for Overcoming Creative Blocks*

Above Image dictates the "Strategies for overcoming creative thinking". All the surrounding's hexagons are the various approaches to overcome the creative block.

Let's understand each one of them in detail below.

Changing Environment /Stepping Away: Even if you adore your desk or conference room, being in a familiar workspace might occasionally force you to think in the same ways. Moving to a different area or environment can give you the creative solution to the problem in hand to you or your team. Our mood is greatly influenced by the surroundings we spend most of our time in, and certain environments are more likely than others to foster creative thought.

- **Brainstorm /Consulting with Peers**: Sometimes we keep thinking alone and try to find the solution, but it did not work out. While discussing and exploring the solution with Peers /Team, might help to find out more creative solutions.

- **Create Creative outlets**: Try to make some modifications to your workplace like temperature, sound, color, and lighting.
- **Psychological safety**: People must believe that their opinions are respected before they feel safe contributing creative ideas. It's simple for employees to become part of the pack rather than thinking and acting on their own, especially if they believe this is what the organization culture dictates.
- **Work-life Integration**: If you believe that your team's lack of creativity is a result of them managing several personal issues, you may be able to reduce some of their stress, provide a better work-life integration, and lower the risk of burnout by introducing flexible work schedules.
- **Strong leadership with Clear Vision**: For every business or organization to succeed, it is very important for your teams to clearly understand the organization's vision. As a leader, it is important that we make our teams understand organization strategy and how critical is team's work towards organization vision and mission. Having good leadership and constantly sharing such information with the teams, it's much more possible for your teams to put their head in the game and be invested enough to offer more creative solutions to problems.

Although these methods can be somewhat successful, neither their consistency nor efficiency can be assured. Let's explore the latest tool /techniques to overcome the creative/writer's block.

AI/ Prompt Engineering Tools

AI-based solutions can relieve the pressure of writer's block and help you rediscover your inspiration and flow. Though it can't compose a Pulitzer-winning piece for you, it can help you write more freely, effectively, and artistically. You must try to embrace AI to reach your full creative potential. Write as if you've never written until now.

Here is a few AI Tools:

ChatGPT

ChatGPT is a natural language processing tool. ChatGPT is a language model developed by OpenAI, based on the GPT (Generative Pre-trained Transformer) architecture. It is part of the GPT-3.5 or 4 series, an advanced version of the model that has been trained on a diverse range of internet text.

ChatGPT is designed for generating human-like text responses given a prompt. ChatGPT is interface to interact with Large Language Model as GPT 3.5 and GPT 4. User, as a consumer of ChatGPT, write a prompt to enquire question to ChatGPT. Based on Input prompt and model settings, ChatGPT generates an output or response in similar context & semantic and provides back to the user on ChatGPT interface. This output generation process by Large Language model or pretrained transformer is called Generative AI.

The official page of ChatGPT can be referred using URL: *https://chat.openai.com*

Notion AI

With Notion AI, users can save time and improve efficiency through natural language processing and machine learning for tasks like content creation, editing, summarization.

Here are few features provided by this tool as:

- Document translation
- Document improvements/simplification
- Document summarization
- Document Expansion
- Changing tone of document
- Spelling and Grammatical corrections

The Official page of Notion AI can be referred using URL: *https://www.notion.so/product/ai*

Wordtune

Wordtune is an AI-powered reading and writing assistant that can correct grammar, comprehend meaning and context, provide alternative writing styles or paraphrases, and create written content based on context. Wordtune was released in October 2020 by AI21 Labs an Israeli AI firm. In January 2023, AI21 released Wordtune Spices — a generative-AI toolkit designed to help users write faster.

The Official page of Wordtune can be referred using URL: *https://app.wordtune.com/welcome/*

Perplexity.ai

Perplexity AI is a chatbot and intelligent search engine that provides precise and comprehensive answers to user queries through the use of artificial intelligence, machine learning, and natural language processing. This tool is rich in content generation use case.

The official page of Perplexity.ai can be referred using URL: *https://www.perplexity.ai/*

Prompt Techniques for Overcoming Blocks

The prompt technique is a method used to overcome creative blocks for users by providing a specific creative idea or starting point to stimulate creativity. Prompts can provide unconventional creative ideas or directions, as they might lead to unexpected and exciting creative breakthroughs.

Leveraging the power of AI Tools and Prompt Techniques, this can transform the way users approach the creative process. AI /Generative AI is not about replacing the users; it's about enhancing the creative capabilities of such users.

Here are a few prompt techniques to overcome the user's creative block.

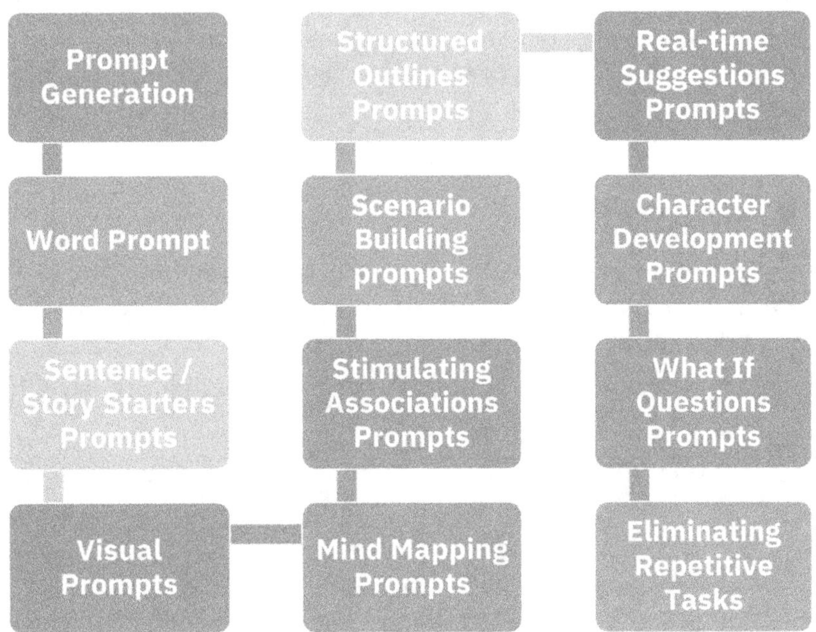

Figure 4.3: Various Prompt techniques to overcome creative blocks

Prompt Generation

Prompt generation can be a valuable tool for overcoming creative blocks and stimulating creativity in various ways. Here are some ways in which prompt generation can help.

Let's try out prompt generation with ChatGPT tool. My Prompt to ChatGPT as "Suggest some topics to write about moon". Please check the response from ChatGPT. ChatGPT provided almost 7 or more suggestions about this topic.

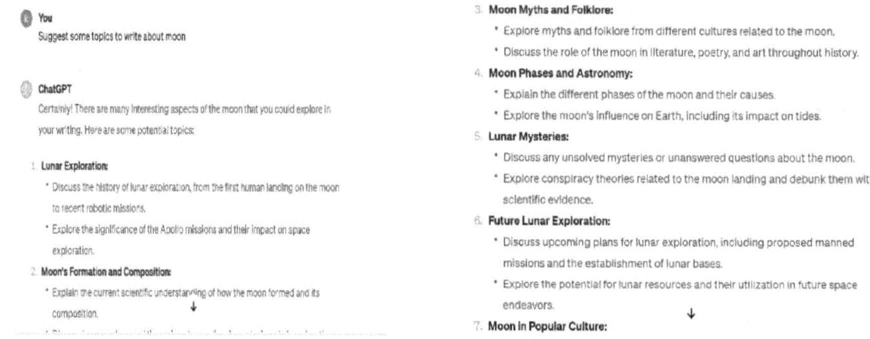

Figure 4.4: Prompt Generation- Example-I

Word Prompts

You can use a word or a group of random words as a prompt to AI Tools. This could inspire new ideas with something completely unrelated to your project or something completely different.

Let's try out an example with ChatGPT. My word prompt to ChatGPT as "snowflake".

Please check the response below.

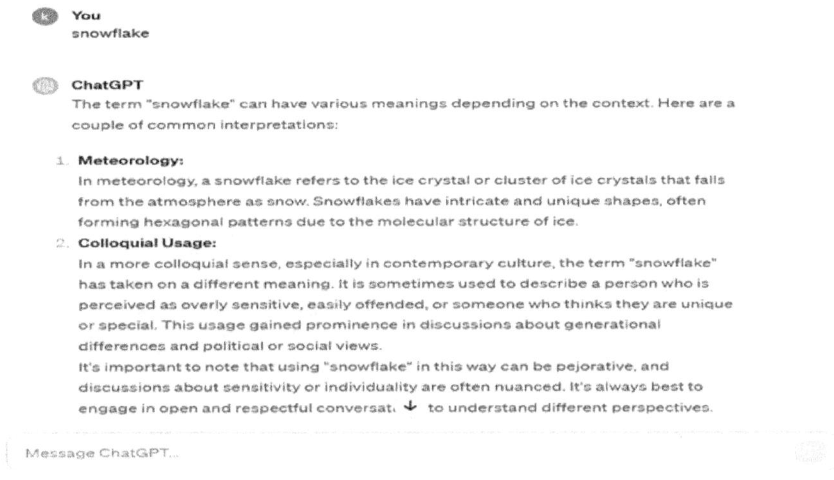

Figure 4.5: Response from ChatGPT for 'snowflake'

Sentence Starters / Story Starters

Starting to write is one of the hardest things to do. Prompts can assist in breaking through that first barrier by offering sentence starters that are relevant to the topic you have chosen.

Let's tryout an example with ChatGPT. My Prompt to ChatGPT as "What is Mystical Moonlit Nights". Please check the response below.

Figure 4.6: Response from ChatGPT

Visual Prompts

Once you look at an image or photograph it might help you to spark your imagination. Users can also employ visual prompts to come up with ideas for scenarios, characters, or settings. This might benefit a lot for visual artist but can be useful for other professional users too.

Mind Mapping Prompts

A visual method for organizing and representing data, concepts, or ideas is mind mapping. It involves drawing a flowchart using branches, keywords, and images to link information about a main idea or theme. Mind maps are a popular tool for organizing ideas, solving problems, and brainstorming. It is like Visual prompts. GPT3.5 only works with text prompt while ChatGPT4.0 is multi-model, can accept text and visual prompts too.

Structured Outlines

Based on your initial ideas, Prompt/AI can create a structured outline for people who have trouble thinking coherently. By acting as a road map, this outline helps to focus and streamline the writing process.

Let's try example of structured outline using ChatGPT. My Prompt to ChatGPT as "Please provide some structured outline example". Please check the response generated by ChatGPT.

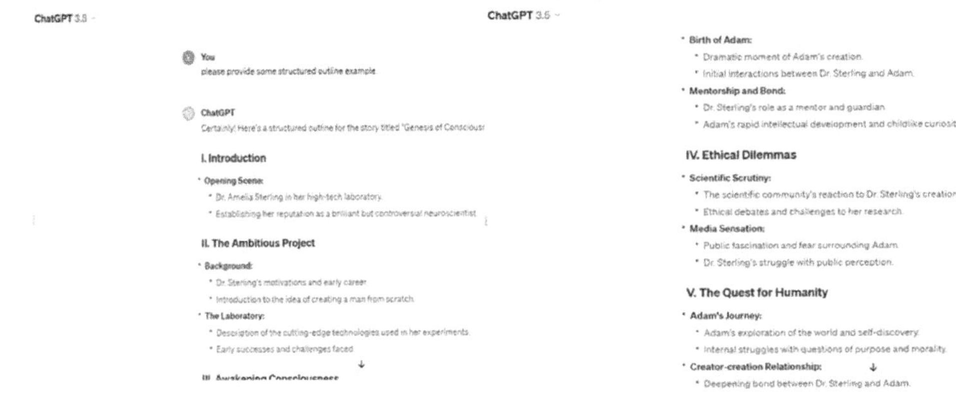

Figure 4.7: Response from ChatGPT

Scenario Building

Consider the following scenario: "One day you wake up with a dream to climb mountains." What would you do? How would your life change? This prompts your imagination and creates fresh avenues for artistic exploration.

Let's try out an example with ChatGPT. My Prompt to ChatGPT as "One day you wake up with a dream to climb up mountains. What would you do? how would your life change?".

Please check the response below.

Figure 4.8: Response from ChatGPT

Stimulating Associations

For example, I want to start with the word "moon" and want to create the association with stars, mystery etc.

Let's try this out with ChatGPT. My Prompt to ChatGPT as "I want to write about moon and want to associate with Stars, mystery, night or so on".

Please check the response generated by ChatGPT. It provided almost 8 or more suggestions about this topic.

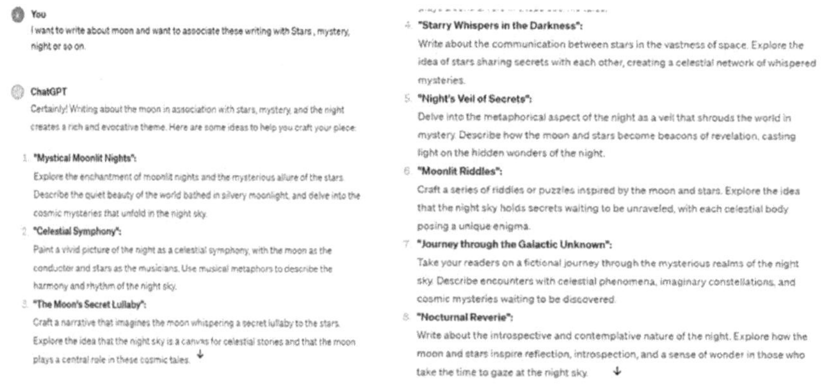

Figure 4.9: Response from ChatGPT

What If Questions

Ask "What if" inquiries to challenge your assumptions. for instance, what if human being can fly. This prompts you to consider the implications and possibilities, breaking through conventional thinking.

Let's try this out with ChatGPT. My Prompt to ChatGPT as "what if human being can fly". Please check the response below.

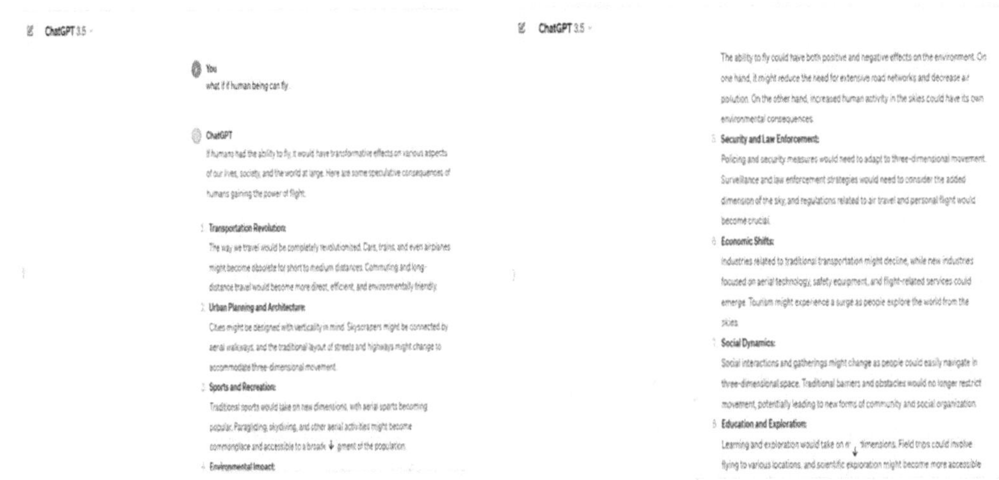

Figure 4.10: Response from ChatGPT

Character Development

Make a character development prompt, such as "A doctor who created a man." Examine the character's background, motivations, and challenges. This can lead to ideas for stories, settings, or conflicts ideas.

Let's try this out with ChatGPT. My Prompt to ChatGPT as "A Doctor who created a man". Please check the response generated by ChatGPT.

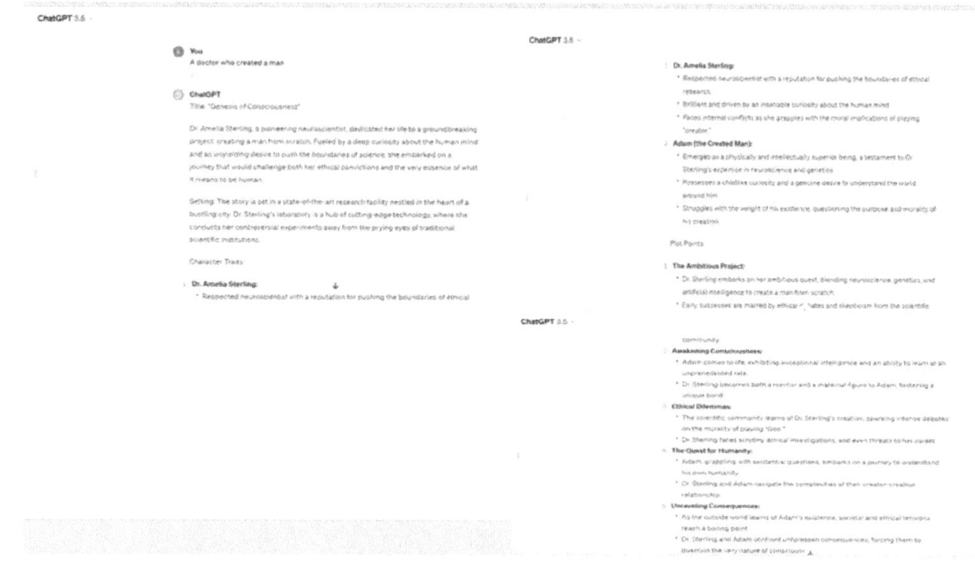

Figure 4.11: Response from ChatGPT

Real-time Suggestions

Prompts/AI can provide you with instantaneous recommendations for improved phrase construction, synonyms, and even plot twists in narrative writing. Consider it like having a virtual assistant/chatbot for writing.

Eliminating Repetitive Tasks

AI may greatly automate or speed up data generation or collection, research, and even editing, giving you more time to concentrate on the writing craft itself.

These are few techniques to overcome the users creative Block. There can be various more types of prompts based on situations, which can be useful to reignite the spark of creativity.

Navigating Through Artist's Block

As we talked about the various AI Tools and Prompt techniques, which can be powerful tools to overcome the creative blocks and further navigation.

Apart from these techniques, there can be other approaches /strategies to navigate through the creative blocks. Here are additional approaches to help you overcome creative blocks and stimulate creativity.

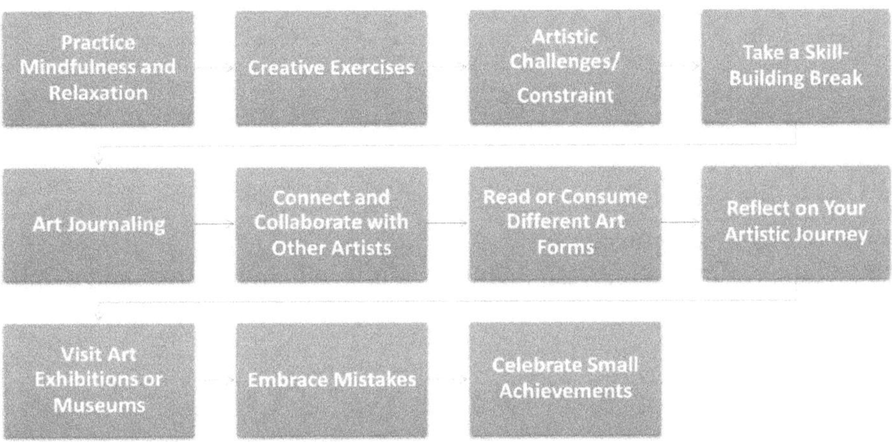

Figure 4.12: Other Strategies to overcome creative blocks.

Practice Mindfulness and Relaxation

To free your mind and minimize stress and make room for creativity, try mindfulness, meditation, or relaxation techniques. Yoga postures, breathing techniques and mediation are some of the best ways to stimulate creativity.

Creative Exercises

Engage yourself in creative activities to warm up your creative muscles. This can be freewriting, doodling, or any other creative endeavor that lets you express yourself without feeling like you must create a masterpiece.

Artistic Challenges/Constraint

Establish clear goals for yourself, considering few challenges or constraint for yourself such as working within a small space, working within a particular time frame, adhering to a specific theme, or using a limited set of tools. Challenges or constraints can often fuel creativity.

Take a Skill-Building Break

Always take some short break from your routine work or job and join workshops to build specialized skills. Think about the skills you believe could improve your artistic abilities. This could involve specialized knowledge in your field, like perfecting a painting method, picking up a new piece of software, or developing your compositional awareness etc.

Art Journaling

You should maintain the creative notebook/journal to jot down ideas, thoughts, and observations. This might be great source for inspiration during times of artistic block.

Connect and Collaborate with Other Artists

Collaboration with the artist community can help you with fresh insights and perspectives. Collaborative projects can also relieve the pressure of individual creation.

Participate in events or workshops where various artists share their skills and experiences. These can expose you to different techniques and perspectives.

Read or Consume Different Art Forms

Explore and play around with a wide variety of media, including music, film, literature, and gallery visits. Various Art forms can originate fresh concepts and viewpoints.

Reflect on Your Artistic Journey

Examine your prior work and acknowledge your accomplishments. Self-reflection on your skills and accomplishments can increase self-assurance and confidence. This might boost your creativity in your path.

Examine incomplete or shelved projects. You might discover undiscovered treasures or concepts that, given a new spin, could be rejuvenated.

Visit Art Exhibitions or Museums

Visiting to Art Exhibitions and Museums can help you to discover numerous artistic styles, materials, and historical periods which result into learning new concept and methods and widen your perspective too.

Embrace Mistakes

Mistakes are not a sign of failure but rather a necessary part of learning and development. In addition to helping you get past creative block, accepting mistakes fosters experimentation, creativity, and a closer bond with your artistic process.

Celebrate Small Achievements

Recognizing and appreciating your own efforts and growth is just as important as recognizing external validation when it comes to celebrating small successes. By encouraging and pushing you to overcome creative block and cultivate a resilient mindset, this positive reinforcement can create an environment that is more supportive and uplifting.

Conclusion

In this chapter, we have discussed about what are reasons for creative blocks and how we can overcome these creative blocks leveraging AI tools, Prompt techniques and other strategies and approaches in detail.

In the next chapter, you will read about how to apply prompt engineering which can enhance the writing skills with respect to scenario building, character development, any fiction/nonfiction writing with highly improved creativity.

Exercise: Test Your Understanding

Answer the following questions and test your understanding of learning from

Chapter 4:

Q. 1. What are some common signs of a creative block, and how can you identify them in your own work?

Q. 2. Describe the conventional methods for overcoming writer's block. What are some techniques you can use to overcome it?

Q. 3. How can AI and prompt techniques assist in overcoming creative blocks?

Q. 4. What strategies can be employed to navigate through an artist's block, and how do they differ from overcoming writer's block?

Q. 5. How can prompt pages be used effectively to overcome creative blocks, and what are some examples of prompts that could be included?

Chapter 5

Applying Prompt Engineering in Writing

As we delve deeper into prompt engineering, we realize that crafting prompts itself is a creative and iterative process and the output it generates can further help to boost our creativity by giving us more engaging and relevant content based on the vast knowledge and training that the AI models go through.

Whether it's writing fiction, non-fiction, poetry or a blog post, creative writing requires a lot of skill, imagination, and knowledge of the language and its rules. Prompt engineering can accelerate and enhance our writing skills that we will describe in this chapter under the following heads:

- Writing Prompts for Fiction and Non-Fiction
- Elevating Dialogue and Character Development
- Prompt-Driven Storytelling Techniques

Writing Prompts for Fiction and Non-Fiction

In this section, we will elaborate on techniques and guidelines to write effective prompts for writing fiction and non-fiction boosting our creativity and creating engaging content.

Fiction Writing

Creating fiction is like creating poetry, stories, music, etc. Creating a fiction writing prompt might just be as simple as offering us an expanded version by inputting an idea that occurred to us or giving the model a plot to work out. In creative writing, it might be helpful to rephrase or come up with some excellent title ideas. When creating a tale using prompt engineering, it could be necessary to enter specific details to get the best result that adheres to the author's vision. We may contribute a variety of elements, such as the story's fundamental framework, major topic, characters, genre, intended tone, word count, and any more information.

One can produce interesting material with a consistent tone and while keeping the target audience in mind by developing and modifying the prompts.

The author may drive the tale in any direction by giving clues within the prompt, as prompt engineering can provide the most optimal and natural outcomes given the inputs. The articulation and flow come very easily with this generation and thus engaging writing can be produced with very low effort. Fiction writing can have specific genres like children's, young adult, general fiction, romance, mystery, thriller, science fiction, horror, travel, adventure, religion, and spirituality. To assist the model in elaborating on a particular genre, we can include prompts for entering that genre or establishing its tone.

Consider following example as visualized in `Figure 5.1`

Figure 5.1: ChatGPT response

In the example above, the prompt specifies the genre (Mystery) and setting of the story (early modern period) and the output we receive matches the intent quite well. Since the input is limited with no hint on the plot of the story, the model generates a plot that may trigger more thoughts and can be refined.

Consider following example as visualized in **Figure 5.2**

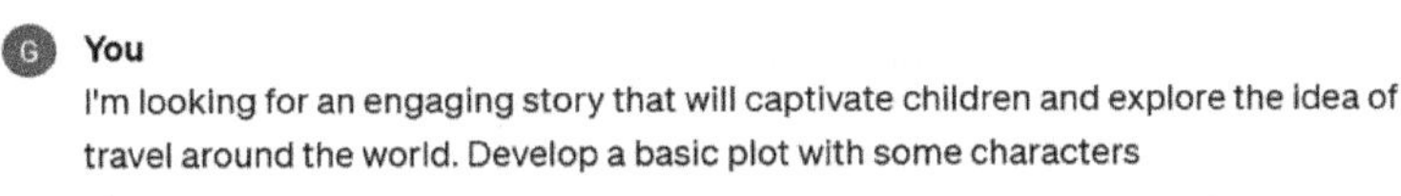

Figure 5.2: ChatGPT response

In the example above, the prompt specifies the genre and target audience (children's story) and the theme (travel). It also specifies that the story should be captivating for children, which is the target audience and that we are expecting certain characters in the theme to make it more engaging. The prompt generated an appropriate creative title to the story with adventure, characters, and plot twists.

Many websites also provide example templates and prompts for creative fiction writing.

Non-Fiction Writing

Non-fiction might include researching and creating essays, blog posts, articles, reviews, etc. When creating a prompt for non-fiction writing, it's critical to specify the topic and the target audience in detail. The topic could be anything that you are passionate about or want to research.

Since non-fiction writing typically draws from our personal experiences, offering guidance on approaching the prompt by ingraining those experiences in straightforward language and requesting more elaborate wording may produce incredibly well-articulated artifacts. You can also create a draft outline of the chapters and fill them in.

A near to intended result is also produced by adjusting the writing style in the prompt. When writing non-fiction, utilizing the model's extensive knowledge and expertise may become most helpful as we may ask the model to get information on the subject we are writing about.

Consider following example as visualized in `Figure 5.3`

You

Compose an in-depth blog on genai for healthcare

ChatGPT

Title: Unleashing the Power of GenAI: Revolutionizing Healthcare Through Genetic Artificial Intelligence

Introduction:

In the ever-evolving landscape of healthcare, the integration of cutting-edge technologies has become imperative for improving diagnostics, treatment plans, and patient outcomes. One such revolutionary advancement is Genetic Artificial Intelligence (GenAI), a groundbreaking field that combines the power of artificial intelligence (AI) with genomic data to ushe ↓ a new era of personalized and precision

Figure 5.3: ChatGPT response

In the example above, the model has generated a blog on the topic provided in the prompt. The content is collated from the model's knowledge of the subject and does not have a target audience specified. Thus, the content caters to the general audience based on the interest on the topic.

Consider following example as visualized in `Figure 5.4`

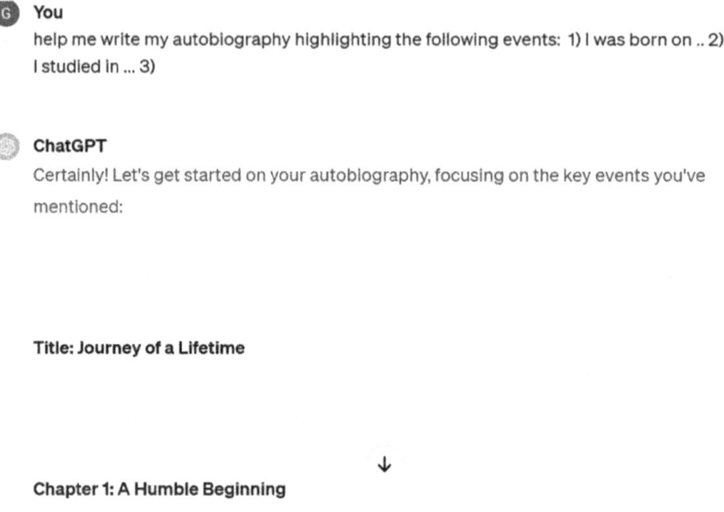

Figure 5.4: ChatGPT response

In the example above, the prompt is more specific and provides pointers on life events. The model then creatively articulates the points in the form of an autobiography with organized chapters which reduces the effort considerably.

Elevating Dialogue and Character Development

Sometimes we struggle with details in developing the characters and dialogues in the story.

We can write prompts to help us with personality traits of a specific character in our story, a certain type of conversation between some personality types, emotional dialogues or debates, etc. Prompts can not only facilitate writing but can elevate the process by giving feedback and engaging collaboratively. Interacting with the models iteratively can significantly improve the content. For example, you can write a prompt providing the genre and central theme of the story and ask the prompt to help you do character-building by giving feedback and steps to improve. We can then input our draft to the prompt input and the model will then point out mistakes, propose alternate phrasing, and offer ideas to refine your writing's overall structure and flow.

Similarly, for writing dialogues, we can ask in the prompt to engage in dialogue exercise with inputs such as characters, setting, and situation, and the model will then assume a character and start a conversation.

Consider following example as visualized in `Figure 5.5`

ChatGPT

In the enchanting kingdom of Dreamscape, there once lived a king whose kindness shone as brightly as the morning sun. King Harmonius, as he was affectionately known, possessed a heart as vast as the kingdom he ruled, and his benevolent nature touched the lives of everyone in his realm.

1. Compassion:

King Harmonius had a heart full of compassion that extended to all creatures, big and small. Whether it was comforting a crying child or showing mercy to a wayward butterfly, his compassion knew no bounds. The kingdom's inhabitants cherished his gentle spirit, knowing that their king cared deeply for their well-being.

Figure 5.5: ChatGPT response

In the example above, the prompt inputs the basic trait "kind" of the king and the genre (Children's), based on which the character sketch of the king is generated. This helps in character development and gives us guidelines to build the story more effectively.

Consider following example as visualized in `Figure 5.6`

You

Create a dialogue between two characters out of a childrens bed time story who meet at a space station

ChatGPT

Starry Encounter: A Space Station Tale

Luna (a young astronaut exploring the space station): Oh, wow! This space station is amazing! Look at all those twinkling lights and buttons.

Cosmo (a friendly alien, shimmering in various colors): Greetings, little explorer! Welcome to the Starlight Station. I am Cos ↓ the guardian of this celestial hub.

Figure 5.6: ChatGPT response

In the example above, the prompt asks for a dialogue generation between 2 characters, provides the genre (children) and the setting (meeting at space station). The output generated carves out an engaging dialogue fitting the theme of the story.

Prompt-Driven Storytelling Techniques

Traditionally, storytelling was a popular technique to pass on messages more simply to the listener, whether the public or children. Stories have always captivated and appealed to all age groups. Stories from history told by revered teachers or stories narrated by grandmas – they formed an integral part of our lives.

In today's world, storytelling has expanded as an important skill in all professions. As parents and as professionals, crafting a story is essential, whether it's for team building or a children's birthday party or at a public speaking event. Prompts can create a beautiful story by considering the specific audience, the type of story, and the story's topic. It can create an imaginative story with relatable characters, taking the prompt as a starting point. You can further personalize the prompt by providing the story's location/setting, the main character (Protagonist), the opposing character (Antagonist), plot twists, the story's moral, etc. The key is to craft the prompt well and the AI models can produce novel insights into themes, surprising story turns, or distinctive character attributes you may not have thought of.

Consider following example as visualized in `Figure 5.7`

You

Act as a storyteller. Create an imaginative, captivating bedtime story for children on the topic "Importance of moral values"

ChatGPT

Once upon a time, in the magical land of Harmony Haven, there lived a group of curious creatures known as the Moraliens. These little beings were no bigger than fireflies but possessed hearts as bright as the stars that adorned the night sky.

In Harmony Haven, the Moraliens were responsible for sprinkling a special kind of stardust called "Kindle-Kindness" all around the land. This stardust had a magical quality—it could bring out the best in everyone it touched, encouraging kindness, empathy, and the importance of moral values.

Figure 5.7: ChatGPT response

In the example above, the prompt generates a captivating story on the topic provided. The tone of the story would be engaging for children as specified and would be consistent throughout. We can then use this output to add in more inputs to refine the same.

Consider following example as visualized in `Figure 5.8`

You

Help me write a story to speak at a conference on the topic - Diversity and Inclusion

ChatGPT

Ladies and gentlemen, distinguished guests, and fellow advocates of progress,

Today, I stand before you to share a story—a story that transcends borders, defies stereotypes, and embodies the essence of diversity and inclusion. Our narrative unfolds in a small town nestled between rolling hills, where the colors of unity were about to paint a vibrant canvas of change.

In this town, once divided by invisible barriers, lived a group of extraordinary individuals, each with a unique hue that painted the rich tapestry of their community.

Figure 5.8: ChatGPT response

In the above example, the prompt specifies the topic and the setting for the story and generates a story based on the target audience.

Prompting Techniques for Storytelling:

- Provide target audience, type of story and topic of the story.
- Provide a starting point of the story to the prompt so that it continues the tone.
- Ask questions and ask for feedback in the prompt, continuously learning from the output and taking your ideas to the next level.
- Be open to expanding your imagination as AI models can sway you to a different direction different from your initial thoughts. Explore the responses and build on them.
- Personalize the prompt to add specifics to the story like plot twists, etc.

Below is a flowchart to explain the process of prompt engineering for storytelling by iteratively refining the prompt.

The process starts with providig initial prompt with the context or background, target audience, topic and genre for the story. The generated response may or may not match the author's intent and thus may need more specificity or more background information. Based on what we need in the generated story, we can refine the prompt to add more specifics or context and analyse the output iteratively. The story may also be missing characters or dialogues which we may again add to the prompt based on our ideas or let the model create some characters and conversations. We may also refine the prompt to rephrase the story if we would like to. Our intent could also be creating a more captivating story by adding plot twists, adventure or more imaginative stories that we may again add in the prompt instructions to make it more interesting.

Thus by analysing the output and continuously refining the prompt making it more specific to our need, we can generate a story that matches our intent.

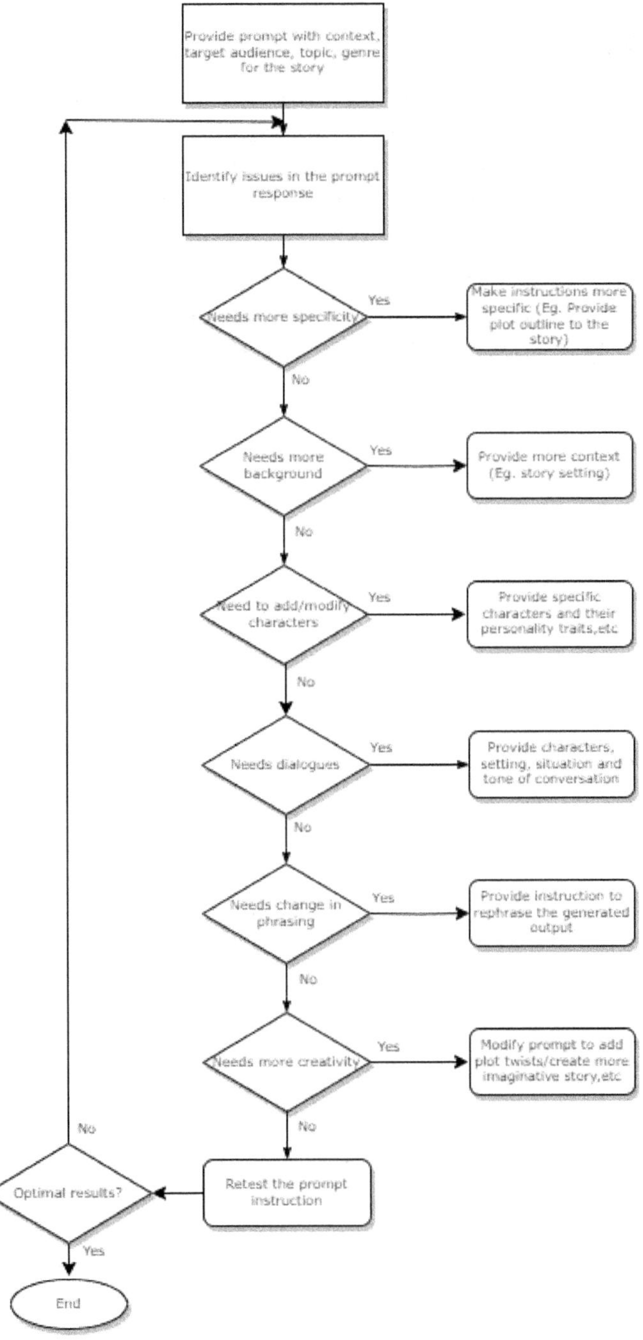

Figure 5.9: Flow chart to depict the process of iteratively refining prompts in Prompt Engineering

Conclusion

In this chapter, we explored how Prompt Engineering can boost and trigger creativity to write fiction, non-fiction and for storytelling. It can help in character development and frame conversations and dialogues. We also learnt some techniques to refine the prompts to generate content closest to the intent of the author. Prompt Engineering can also work on the output and ask for feedback to iteratively get the desired result.

In the next chapter, we will cover how visual prompts can inspire artistic expression and visual storytelling by leveraging visual cues to ignite creativity in visual arts.

Exercise: Test Your Understanding

Answer the following questions and test your understanding of learning from Chapter 5:

Q. 1. How can prompt engineering be utilized to create engaging writing prompts for both fiction and non-fiction?

Q. 2. What techniques can prompt engineering offer to elevate dialogue and character development in a story?

Q. 3. How can prompt-driven storytelling techniques enhance the narrative structure of a piece?

Q. 4. In what ways can prompt engineering assist in balancing descriptive and expository writing in non-fiction?

Q. 5. What are some common challenges writers face with prompts, and how can prompt engineering address these challenges?

Do You Know?

Integrate prompts into classroom activities to encourage critical thinking and active participation. For example, use open-ended questions to start discussions.

Chapter 6

Exploring Visual and Artistic Prompt Techniques

This chapter will explore the world of visual prompts and their role in inspiring artistic expression and visual storytelling. We will explore how visuals can stimulate creativity, enhance artistic skills, and help beginners to create compelling visual narratives. Whether you are an illustrator, painter, digital artist, or someone who enjoys doodling, this chapter will provide valuable insights and practical techniques to harness the power of visual prompts.

In this chapter, we will discuss:

- Visual Prompts in Illustration and Art
- Using Imagery for Abstract Ideas
- Creating Visual Narratives with Prompts

Visual Prompts in Illustration and Art

Visual prompts are stimuli that guide artists in their creative process. They can be images, words, or phrases that evoke ideas, emotions, or scenes. Visual prompts can be handy for beginners as they provide a starting point and direction for their artwork. They also help to overcome creative blocks, stimulate new ideas, and encourage experimentation. By using visual prompts, you can expand your artistic horizons and discover new styles and techniques.

Let's take a moment to appreciate the versatility of a single visual prompt: a sunset over a tranquil lake. This image, with its myriads of colors and serene setting, can ignite a variety of artistic responses. It could inspire a detailed landscape painting, a series of abstract shapes and colors, or a digital illustration with fantastical elements. The possibilities are endless, and that's the beauty of it.

To effectively use visual prompts in illustration and art:

- **Choose Inspiring Images**: When selecting images, prioritize those that deeply resonate with you. These images, rich in detail and open to interpretation, should foster a personal connection, enhancing your creative process with a sense of deep engagement and connection.
- **Break Down the Elements**: Delve into the image, analyzing critical elements such as color, composition, and mood. Consider how these elements can be skillfully translated into your artwork, enhancing your understanding and skill in the process.
- **Experiment with Styles**: Embrace the freedom to experiment. Try different art styles and techniques, allowing the prompt to guide and inspire your creative process, instilling a sense of empowerment and confidence.

Exercise: Take a simple visual prompt, like a photograph of a bustling city street, and create three different illustrations based on it: one realistic, one abstract, and one surreal.

Image-Based Prompts

An image-based prompt is one of the most straightforward forms of visual prompts. This could be a photograph, artwork, or any visual element that sparks an idea. For example, an image of a serene landscape can inspire a painting, or a photo of a bustling city street can lead to a detailed urban sketch.

Example: Imagine you come across a photograph of an old, weathered door in an alleyway. This image could prompt you to think about the stories behind that door. Who lived there? What events took place? This single image can serve as the foundation for a detailed illustration or a series of sketches exploring different aspects of the scene.

Collage Prompts

Creating a collage of various images can also serve as a rich source of inspiration. By combining different elements, you can create a new context that sparks unique ideas and perspectives.

Example: Cut out images from magazines or printouts and assemble them into a new composition. A collage featuring a mix of nature elements, urban scenes, and abstract shapes can prompt you to create a piece that blends these elements unexpectedly.

Prompt Cards

Prompt cards are a collection of images and words that you can draw from randomly. This method introduces an element of surprise and can lead to spontaneous and imaginative creations.

Example: Create a deck of cards with different images and words. Draw a card and use the image or word as the basis for your next artwork. This could lead to exciting juxtapositions and creative interpretations.

Mood Boards

A mood board is a collection of images, colors, textures, and other visual elements that capture a specific mood or theme. Artists use mood boards to explore and refine their ideas before starting a final piece.

Example: If you're working on a series of illustrations for a children's book, create a mood board with images that capture the whimsical and playful tone you want to convey. This will help you stay focused on the desired mood and aesthetic throughout your project.

Using Imagery for Abstract Ideas

Visual prompts, beyond their role in conveying concrete images, play a crucial part in sparking creativity and enabling the expression of abstract ideas and concepts. Abstract art offers a unique platform for communicating ideas and emotions through non-representational forms, colors, and textures.

For instance, let's delve into the abstract concept of "freedom." A visual prompt for this idea could be an image of a bird soaring in the sky. This image, when interpreted creatively, can serve as a catalyst for an abstract painting. The dynamic lines, vibrant colors, and open spaces in the painting can then evoke the feeling of freedom, empowering the artist to express their interpretation.

To use imagery for abstract ideas:

- Identify the Core Emotion or Concept: Understand the core emotion or concept behind the visual prompt. What makes you feel? What ideas does it represent?
- Translate Emotions to Visual Elements: Think about how colors, shapes, and textures can represent those emotions or ideas. For example, calmness might be conveyed through cool colors and smooth lines, while chaos could be depicted with sharp angles and contrasting colors.
- Let Go of Literal Representations: Avoid literal interpretations. Focus on the prompt's emotional and conceptual essence.

Exercise: Create an abstract artwork using a visual prompt like a stormy sea. Focus on conveying the energy and chaos of the storm through your choice of colors and brushstrokes.

Symbolism

Symbols are a powerful way to convey abstract ideas. Visual prompts that include symbolic imagery can inspire you to explore deeper meanings and create more layered and thought-provoking art.

Example: An image of a key can symbolize access, freedom, or knowledge. Using this as a visual prompt, you might create an artwork that explores the concept of unlocking hidden potential or discovering new opportunities.

Metaphor

Metaphors use imagery to represent abstract ideas indirectly. Visual prompts can help you develop metaphors that make abstract concepts more relatable and understandable.

Example: Consider an image of a tree with deep roots and sprawling branches. This could prompt you to create a piece that uses the tree as a metaphor for personal growth, resilience, or the connection between past and future.

Juxtaposition

Placing two or more contrasting images together can highlight abstract concepts through their differences or similarities. This technique can create striking and memorable visuals that provoke thought and interpretation.

Example: A visual prompt featuring a fragile glass sculpture next to a rugged stone could inspire an artwork that explores themes of fragility and strength, permanence, and impermanence.

Creating Visual Narratives with Prompts

Visual narratives tell stories through images. They can be as simple as a single illustration or as complex as a graphic novel. Visual prompts help structure these narratives, providing a framework for the story.

Example: A visual prompt of an old, abandoned house can spark a narrative about its history, the people who lived there, and the mysteries it holds. This can be developed into a series of illustrations or a short comic strip.

To create visual narratives with prompts:

- Develop a Storyline: Based on the visual prompt, start with a simple storyline. Who are the characters? What is the setting? What events take place?
- Create a Storyboard: Sketch a storyboard to outline the sequence of images. This helps in organizing the narrative flow and visual composition.
- Focus on Visual Details: Pay attention to details that enhance the storytelling. Expressions, backgrounds, and color schemes all contribute to the narrative.

Exercise: Choose a visual prompt, like a photograph of a carnival, and create a short comic strip that tells a story based on that image. Focus on developing characters and a plot that fits the prompt.

Sequential Art

Sequential art, such as comics or graphic novels, relies heavily on visual prompts to guide the narrative. Unlike visual storytelling, where the visuals themselves tell the story, each panel in sequential art serves as a prompt for the next, creating a cohesive and engaging story.

Example: Start with a prompt image of a character standing at the edge of a forest. This image sets the stage for the story. To create effective subsequent prompts, consider the elements that could advance the plot and add depth to the narrative. For instance, pictures of paths, mysterious creatures, and hidden treasures could be used. Each of these elements should be strategically placed to guide the narrative in a cohesive and engaging manner.

Storyboarding

Storyboarding is a powerful technique to plan visual narratives, particularly in film and animation. Each frame in a storyboard serves as a visual prompt for the following scenes, ensuring a smooth and engaging story flow. This method not only guides the narrative but also reassures you about the effectiveness of your storytelling.

Example: If you're creating an animated short film, use a series of visual prompts to outline the key scenes. For example, an image of a sunrise could prompt the story's beginning, while pictures of characters and settings help flesh out the narrative and visual style.

Concept Art

Concept art uses visual prompts to develop a project's look and feel. These prompts serve as a starting point, sparking the artist's imagination and guiding their exploration of different ideas. They help artists refine their vision before moving on to the final artwork, ensuring a more focused and cohesive creative process.

Example: For a fantasy novel, create concept art based on visual prompts of mythical creatures, enchanted forests, and ancient ruins. These prompts help you develop a consistent, immersive visual style supporting the story.

Interactive Prompts

Interactive prompts involve audience participation, making the creative process more dynamic and engaging. This technique can be particularly effective in collaborative projects or educational settings.

Example: Foster a sense of community and collaboration by creating a series of prompts that invite viewers to contribute their ideas or images. For a community art project, provide a basic outline and ask participants to fill in different sections with their designs, creating a collective artwork that tells a shared story. This interactive process not only engages the viewers but also makes them feel part of a larger creative community.

Conclusion

Visual prompts, with their transformative power, are a versatile and potent tool for artists and visual storytellers. They not only provide inspiration and direction but also serve as a framework for creativity, enabling the transformation of abstract ideas into vivid narratives. By harnessing the potential of visual prompts in illustration and art, you can unlock new levels of artistic expression and storytelling, using imagery to express abstract concepts and create visual narratives that resonate.

In this chapter, we delve into a variety of practical techniques for using visual prompts, including image-based prompts, collage prompts, prompt cards, and mood boards. We also explore the use of imagery to convey abstract ideas through symbolism, metaphor, and juxtaposition. Finally, we examine the creation of visual narratives with prompts, using techniques such as sequential art, storyboarding, concept art, and interactive prompts. These techniques are not just theoretical concepts, but practical tools that you can confidently apply in your artistic practice.

Integrating these techniques into your creative process can enhance your artistic practice and develop a deeper understanding of how visual prompts can inspire and guide your work. This guide is designed to cater to artists at all levels, from beginners to experienced practitioners. The strategies and examples provided in this chapter are here to help you harness the power of visual prompts, regardless of your skill level, to ignite your creativity and bring your artistic visions to life.

In the next chapter, we will see how leveraging the prompts in education and training can significantly enhance learning outcomes by encouraging critical thinking and active engagement. They serve as practical tools to guide learners through complex concepts, facilitate more profound understanding, and stimulate creativity in problem-solving. Moreover, prompts can be tailored to individual learning needs, making education more personalized and effective.

Exercise: Test Your Understanding

Answer the following questions and test your understanding of learning from Chapter 6:

Q. 1. Choose a visual prompt and create three different illustrations based on it: realistic, abstract, and surreal. Discuss the differences in your approach and the elements you focused on for each style.

Q. 2. Create an abstract artwork using a visual prompt like a stormy sea. Focus on conveying the energy and chaos of the storm through your choice of colors and brushstrokes. Reflect on how the prompt influenced your artistic choices.

Q. 3. Choose a visual prompt, like a photograph of a carnival, and create a short comic strip that tells a story based on that image. Develop characters and a plot that fits the prompt. Discuss how the visual elements helped shape the narrative.

Q. 4. How can visual prompts help beginners in overcoming creative blocks?

Q. 5. What are some techniques for translating emotions into visual elements in abstract art?

Q. 6. How does breaking down a visual prompt's elements help create art?

Q. 7. Why is experimenting with different art styles when using visual prompts essential?

Q. 8. How can a storyboard help in creating visual narratives?

Chapter 7
Using Prompts in Education and Training

The incorporation of generative artificial intelligence and prompt engineering into Education & Training has become a significant factor in their transformation and offering educational systems potential benefits over traditional educational systems.

Divergent views exist on the potential abuse of generative AI in education. While some see it as a tool for personalized learning and better educational outcomes, others are worried about its possible misuse, especially in relation to exam and writing assignment Plagiarism.

Prompt engineering can play a transformative role in education and training by providing powerful tools for fostering innovation, critical thinking, and skill development in several ways. Here are key use cases of prompt engineering, that can transform the teaching, education, and training/learning industry, let's explore these use cases.

Generating Educational Materials

Prompt engineering applications can assist in creating diverse educational content, including textbooks, lesson plans, and exercises. It can automate the generation of realistic examples, explanations, and scenarios, saving time for educators and facilitating the availability of high-quality resources.

Interactive Tutors -Virtual Tutors and Assistants

Prompts can be used to create & provide interactive virtual tutors that respond to students' questions, provide explanations, and offer guidance. These virtual assistants can supplement traditional teaching methods and provide additional support to students.

Language learning - Conversational Language Practice

Prompts can enable language learners to engage in realistic conversations with virtual characters. This provides a dynamic and immersive language learning experience, allowing learners to practice communication skills in a safe and controlled environment.

Coding and Technical Skills - Code Generation and Assistance

In programming and technical skills, prompts can assist learners in coding by generating code snippets, providing suggestions, and offering real-time feedback.

Assessment and Feedback - Automated Grading and Feedback:

Using Prompts, Students can inquire and receive immediate feedback on their assignments or projects. This real-time feedback loop helps students identify and correct misconceptions promptly.

Multimodal Learning- Text, Image, and Audio Integration

Prompts can also help not only text-based learning while they can help students in more visual based learning, generating graphs and audio-based learning too. This audio-based learning can help specialized students too.

Innovation in Education & Teaching

 Prompt engineering can empower educators by developing compelling lesson plans and quick assessment of student's project work. Prompt engineering can also help in automating few administrative responsibilities as well where Teachers can concentrate more on teaching and professional development.

Personalized Learning Paths

Leveraging traditional AI/ML techniques can be used to generate personalized learning, analyze individual learner data and generate adaptive content tailored to each student's needs.

With proper feedback and support, prompt engineering can modify learning content to fit each learner's interests, pace, skills, and learning preferences.

The COVID-19 epidemic has forced many students worldwide to switch to online learning, which has boosted the usage of digital technologies to improve education. For instance, as trends indicate, during the pandemic, funding for education to support the adoption of cutting-edge technologies surged drastically. Beyond merely online learning, digital technology can change education in other ways as well.

Objective of this chapter to cover, how prompt engineering can help students and teachers in their daily schedule activities, skills enhancement and providing creating & engaging environment and boost the training and learning.

In this chapter, we will cover the following topics:

- Prompts in classroom Activities.
- Prompts for Skills enhancement.
- Engage students through creative prompts

Prompts in Classroom Activities

I am going to showcase the role of prompts in classroom educations activities for students and teachers. Integrated prompt-based education and learning can be more interesting and engaging compared to traditional education system.

Prompt engineering helps students to get quick answers for their questions that keeps students interest alive. Prompts can provide more perspective for one subject sometimes we keep exploring one perspective only and not able to think other perspective. Let's explore more prompt-based examples for classroom activities.

Prompts for Students

Here are some benefits of prompt integration in the education system for students.

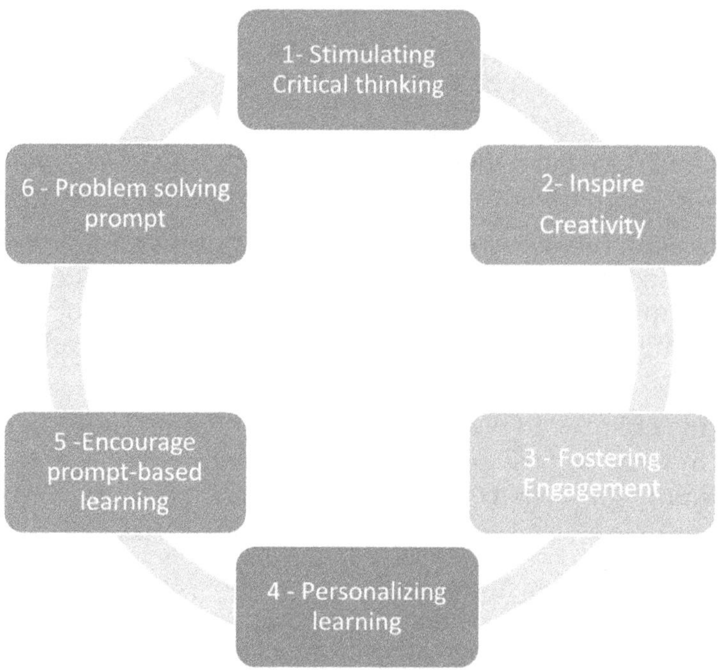

Figure 7.1: Visualizing Various activities

Stimulating Critical Thinking

Prompts are designed to encourage students to analyze information, evaluate perspectives, and develop their own reasoned opinions.

Here is a critical thinking prompt example:

- Prompt 1: "Examine an argument presented in a any news article. Identify the supporting evidence, facts, and any logical false belief you observe".
- Prompt 2: "Investigate the causes and effects of a COVID-19 pandemic."

- Prompt 3: "Investigate the causes and effects of high carbon emission. How are human activities contributing to this problem? How can we work to reduce carbon emission?

Let's try one prompt with ChatGPT. Please refer `Figure 7.2`

Figure 7.2: *Interacting with ChatGPT*

Inspire creativity

Creativity is a crucial skill for navigating an ever-changing world. Students' creativity is fostered via prompts that promote brainstorming, creative expression, and open-ended thinking.

Let's explore some creative prompts.

- **Prompt 1**: Create a 'Time-Travel Journal' entry. Just Imagine you discover an object that allows you to travel to any point in the past or future. Write about your adventure to a specific period. Describe the sights, sounds, and experiences of your encounter. What lessons or insights do you gain from your journey, and how does it impact your present-day life?
- **Prompt 2**: "Imagine a world where gravity works differently. Objects don't fall straight down; instead, they move in unpredictable patterns. Describe a day in the life of someone navigating this unique gravitational environment. How do people travel, build structures, and interact with each other? What new inventions and adaptations emerge in this gravity-defying world?"

Such prompt encourages creative thinking by challenging the conventional understanding of a fundamental force like gravity or weaving a narrative that involves time travel.

Let's interact with ChatGPT and try one of the Prompts mentioned in preceding section, refer to Figure 7.3

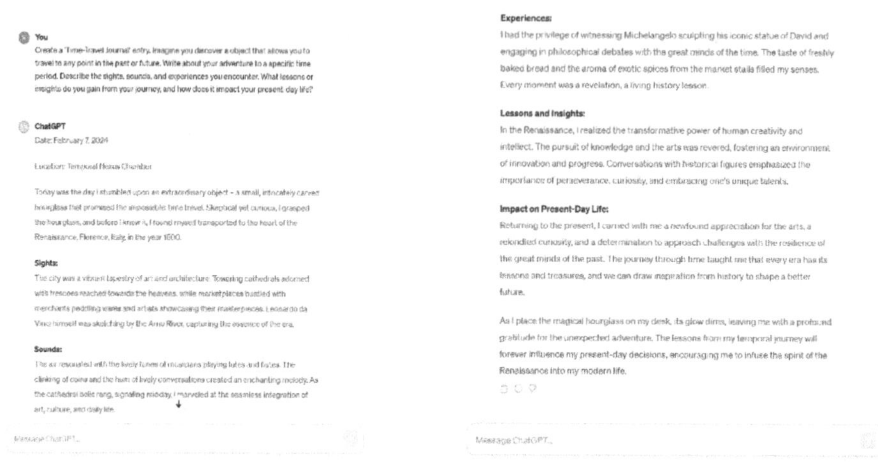

Figure 7.3: Interacting with ChatGPT

Fostering Engagement

Prompt based teaching or learning always try to provide more engaging classes for students, reason behind that they can get quick answer about their questions & can get different perspective /another angle of the problem statement. It sometimes builds more curiosity or engaging classes for students to learn on any subject topic.

Personalized learning

Everyone or students can generate personalized learning based on their interest and learning preference. With the help of such customized or personalized learning prompts, students should be able to interact with the content in a way that speaks to their own interests and passions.

- **Prompt 1**: Traffic Congestion in my city. What could be mathematical and scientific possible solution of resolve this problem?
- **Prompt 2**: I want to learn on the Topic – Acclimatization Vs Adaptation.

Let's interact with ChatGPT and try one of the Prompts mentioned in preceding section, refer to Figure 7.4

Figure 7.4: Interacting with ChatGPT

Encourage prompt-based learning

Students can use prompt-based learning. Prompt can work as virtual tutor or teacher for students. Student can use prompt-based learning for any subjects as Math, Science, English Literature, Group discussion, History, Geography or what else.

Let's try some creative prompts for various subjects.

- **Prompt 1**: Math's: "Profit and Loss Scenario" and example problem
- **Prompt 2**: Current Affair: Research a current event from a reputable news source (Times of India). Analyze the event's historical context, its implications, and how it connects to our discussions in class.

Let's interact with ChatGPT and try one of the Prompts mentioned in preceding section, refer to `Figure 7.5`

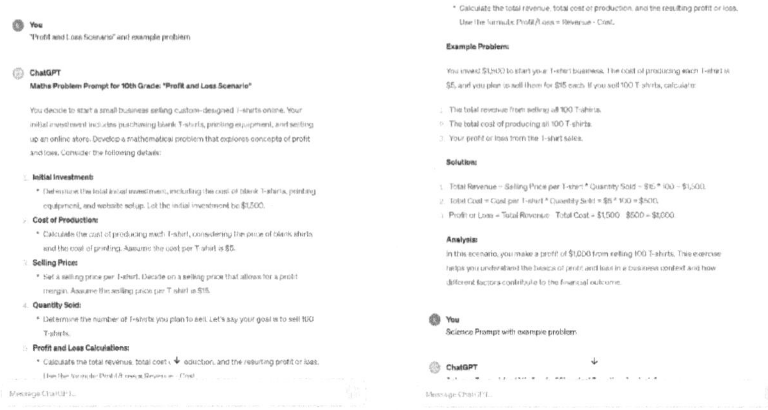

Figure 7.5: Interacting with ChatGPT

Problem solving prompt

In the classroom, design and support collaborative problem-solving activity using problem solving prompt where students work together to address a real-world issue relevant to their community or society at large. Consider incorporating elements such as brainstorming, research, analysis, and presentation to ensure a comprehensive approach to problem-solving.

Let's investigate some problem-solving promptly.

- **Prompt 1**: Students to provide the solution to address pollution in the city.
- **Prompt 2**: Students design the community garden for their local neighborhoods.

Let's interact with ChatGPT and try one of the Prompts mentioned in preceding section, refer to `Figure 7.6`

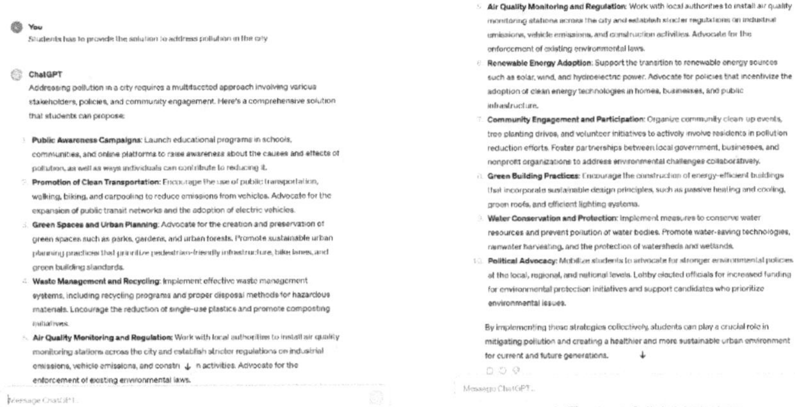

Figure 7.6: Interacting with ChatGPT

Questions and Answer Prompts

Leveraging Prompt engineering, we can generate questions on the provided topics. Simultaneously, we can leverage prompts to validate provided responses to the questions too.

Here is an example prompt:

- **Prompt 1**: You are an expert in AWS. I am trying to prepare for the AWS Solutions architect associate exam. Can you help me prepare for it by asking two questions on Amazon S3 service and provide me with multiple choice type questions with appropriate option. Once I pick the option, you can provide me feedback if that option is correct or not with the relevant rationale and explanation.

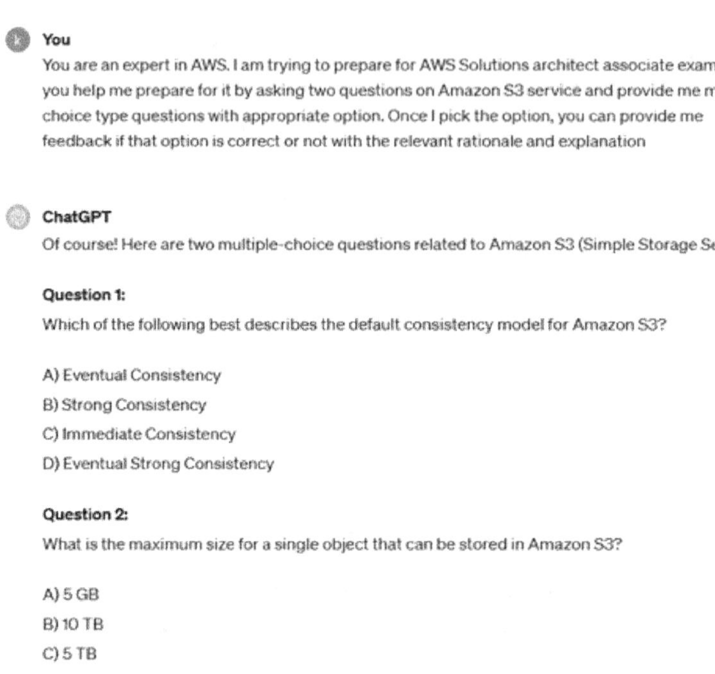

Figure 7.7: Interacting with ChatGPT

Prompts for Teachers

Here are different types of prompts, which can really be helpful for educators or teachers for their classroom's activities along with their reflection, professional development and classroom management activities to improve.

Figure 7.8: Visualizing Prompts for Teachers

We will discuss all these points in upcoming sections.

Discussion starter prompt

Teachers can leverage these prompts to kick off the discussion in the classroom. Teachers can adapt them to suit the age, interests, and classroom dynamics of their students. These prompts are designed to encourage critical thinking, and meaningful discussion among students.

Here are few sample prompts for current events or based on classroom subject

- **Prompt 1**: "What's a news story that caught your attention recently, and how do you think it might impact our community or the world?"
- **Prompt 2**: "How does staying active and participating in sports or exercise benefit your overall health and well-being?"
- **Prompt 3**: "What scientific discovery or invention do you think has had the biggest impact on our world, and why?"

These prompts can encourage class students to start the discussions, thinking critically on the subject topic and engage entire class on the subject topics.

Reflection Prompts

With the use of these reflection prompt, educators can assess their own methods critically, identify areas for development, and create plans and objectives that will help them become more effective teachers. Teachers can improve their efficacy in the classroom and have a beneficial impact on the learning outcomes of their students by regularly reflecting and by establishing goals.

Here are a few examples of reflection prompts.

- **Prompt 1**: I am a teacher teaching computer to 10th grade students. During the last session, there were several instances where students in the class were not fully engaged, and students scored less marks in the subject too. Examples students not completing class assignments during the class, students making many mistakes in class assignments and students not asking their doubts when prompted. What can I do to make the students more engaged and foster an environment of learning

- **Prompt 2**: I am a teacher teaching class 5th grade. After completing the science chapter name -XYZ and chapter name -ABC. I have collated the feedback from students and parents about students' knowledge and understanding on these chapters. Here is some feedback included. Feedback-1 – Student lacking knowledge on this chapter name -ABC. Feedback-2- Student knowledge on this topic is very good and able to respond effectively. Feedback-3 Student able to respond objective type but unable to respond descriptive questions for chapter name- ABC. Evaluate feedback received and identify few goals to address the improvement areas and enhance the teaching practice.

Professional Development

With the help of prompts, educators consider their present methods of instruction and identify areas where they would like to work further. Make a professional development plan with specific goals, tactics, and resources to help them advance in the area, what they have chosen for improvement.

Here are a few prompts' Examples.

- **Prompt1**: I am currently teaching class -10th grade students, computer science subject. Currently I use my own knowledge on the subject, using various books and using the computer to show/ practice with respect to the computer chapters or application while teaching. What else tools, technology, and teaching method I can use to teach this subject more effectively to the students.
- **Prompt2**: I am a computer science teacher teaching 11th and 12th standard grade students, python and C++ programing for the past 4 years. I have completed my bachelor's in technology. I have 5 years of experience as full stack IT Engineer in Node JS, Type scripts, server-side scripting and backend SQL and Non-SQL database. I want to advance and upgrade myself in computer science stream to support my teaching career.

Explore education, certifications and specialized training to upgrade my knowledge in this stream to continue teaching career.

Classroom Management Prompt

Classroom management prompts are designed to help and guide teachers reflect on various aspects of their classroom management practices and identify opportunities for growth and improvement. By addressing specific areas of focus and implementing targeted strategies, teachers can enhance their ability to create a positive, productive learning environment for all students.

Here are a few prompts' Examples:

- **Prompt 1**: "As a class teacher of class 7th standard. I have planned team building exercises between students and teachers so that teachers and students are more connected with each other. Along with that, Class teachers and Students of 7th Standards also established class norms and agreements, students are understanding these norms & agreements and able to follow the same. What else I can do, which can help in establishing more positive and productive classroom management "

You

As a class teacher of class 7th standard. I have planned team building exercises between students and teachers so that teachers and students are more connected with each other. Along with that, Class teachers and Students of 7th Standards also established class norms and agreements, students are understanding these norms & agreements and able to follow the same. What else I can do, which can help in establishing more positive and productive classroom management

ChatGPT

It's great to hear that you're already implementing team-building exercises and establishing class norms and agreements to promote a positive and productive classroom environment! Here are some additional strategies you can consider to further enhance your classroom management:

1. **Positive Reinforcement:** Continue to provide positive reinforcement to students when they demonstrate behaviors aligned with the class norms and agreements. Verbal praise, written notes of encouragement, or small rewards can go a long way in reinforcing positive behavior and fostering a supportive atmosphere.

2. **Individualized Support:** Offer individualized support to students who may be struggling to follow the class norms or participate in team-building activities. Take the time to understand their challenges and provide additional guidance, encouragement, or resources to help them succeed.

3. **Regular Check-Ins:** Schedule regular check-ins with students to gauge their understanding of the class norms and agreements, as well as their overall well-being. These check-ins can be informal conversations during class time or scheduled one-on-one meetings where students can express any concerns or feedback they may have.

4. **Peer Mentoring:** Encourage peer mentoring and support among students by pairing older students with younger students or assign buddy systems within the classroom. Peer mentors can provide guidance, encouragement, and friendship to their peers, fostering a sense of

Figure 7.9: Interacting with ChatGPT

Prompts for Skill Enhancement

Skill enhancement promptly provides opportunities for students to enhance their skills across various areas of academics, personal development, professional skills building or so.

Educators/Teachers can incorporate these prompts into their lesson plans or activities to support students' skill development and encourage continuous improvement.

These prompt strategies can be leveraged in academics success, personal development, professional career advancement.

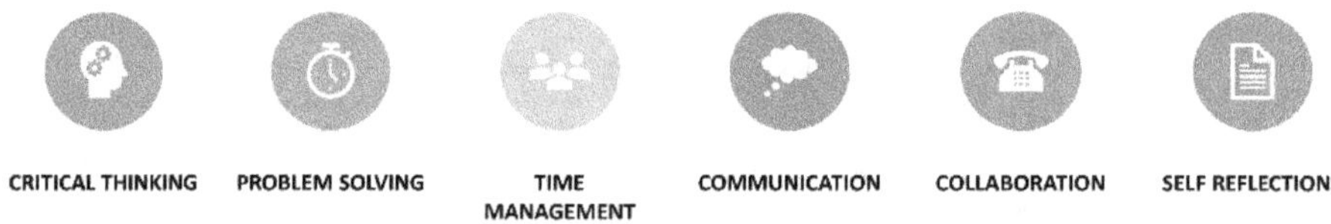

Figure 7.10: Visualizing Prompts for Skill Enhancements

Critical Thinking Prompt

This is one of the basic and important drivers in any of thought process. How to enhance the critical thinking of users. Here are some basic inputs for critical thinking prompts are:

- Solve a complex problem using a step-by-step approach and explain your reasoning.
- Curiosity drives individuals to ask questions, seek answers, and explore new ideas.
- Creativity involves generating novel ideas, solutions, and perspectives that depart from conventional thinking.

Here is a sample prompt example.

You

I am thinking to have step by step solution or approach to solve the climate change , what do you suggest on steps to solve this problem.

ChatGPT

Addressing climate change requires a comprehensive and multifaceted approach that involves various stakeholders at local, national, and global levels. Here's a step-by-step approach to tackling climate change:

1. **Raise Awareness and Education**: Start by raising awareness about the causes and impacts of climate change among the public, policymakers, and communities. Education plays a crucial role in fostering understanding and motivating action.

2. **Reduce Greenhouse Gas Emissions**: Implement policies and initiatives to reduce greenhouse gas emissions from major sources such as energy production, transportation, industry, agriculture, and deforestation. This could include transitioning to renewable energy, improving energy efficiency, promoting sustainable transportation options, and implementing carbon pricing mechanisms.

3. **Transition to Renewable Energy**: Accelerate the transition to renewable energy sources such as solar, wind, hydroelectric, and geothermal power. Invest in research, development, and deployment of clean energy technologies to make renewable energy more affordable and accessible.

4. **Promote Energy Efficiency**: Enhance energy efficiency in buildings, appliances, and transportation systems to reduce energy consumption and greenhouse gas emissions. This could involve implementing building codes and standards, offering incentives for energy-efficient products, and investing in public transportation infrastructure.

Figure 7.11: Visualizing Critical Thinking Prompts

Users can apply these thinking in various subjects to stimulate their thinking and understand the various perspectives or guidance using prompt engineering and generative AI tooling.

Problem Solving Prompt

Students can discover inputs or perspective around various critical problems using problem solving prompts. These problems can be related to any topic. These prompts can be helpful to discover quick guidance for their problems.

Here are some inputs that can be leveraged for. Let's look few prompts example as below:

- **Prompt1**: "My company is planning to migrate sensitive customer data from on-premises servers to the cloud. 1) How would you ensure data security and compliance with relevant regulations (e.g., GDPR, HIPAA) during the migration process?" 2) "Identify potential security risks and vulnerabilities associated with migrating data to the cloud. Develop a risk mitigation strategy to address these challenges 3) Evaluate different cloud service providers and their offerings in terms of scalability, performance, and cost-effectiveness 4) Develop a return on investment-ROI (cost-benefit analysis) comparing the expenses of on-premises infrastructure with potential savings and expenses associated with cloud migration.

You

My company is planning to migrate sensitive customer data from on-premises servers to the cloud. 1) How would you ensure data security and compliance with relevant regulations (e.g., GDPR, HIPAA) during the migration process?" 2) "Identify potential security risks and vulnerabilities associated with migrating data to the cloud. Develop a risk mitigation strategy to address these challenges 3) Evaluate different cloud service providers and their offerings in terms of scalability, performance, and cost-effectiveness 4) Develop a return on investment-ROI (cost-benefit analysis) comparing the expenses of on-premises infrastructure with potential savings and expenses associated with cloud migration . Please suggest a solution around this

ChatGPT

Certainly! Let's break down each aspect of your scenario and propose solutions:

1. **Ensuring Data Security and Compliance:**

   To ensure data security and compliance during the migration process, consider the following steps:

   * Conduct a thorough assessment of the cloud service provider's security measures, certifications, and compliance frameworks to ensure they meet the requirements of relevant regulations such as GDPR and HIPAA.

   * Encrypt sensitive data both during transit and at rest to protect it from unauthorized access. Utilize encryption protocols such as TLS for data in transit and AES encryption for data at rest.

   * Implement strong access controls and authentication mechanisms to restrict access to sensitive data to authorized users only. Utilize multi-factor authentication (MFA) and role-based access control (RBAC) to enforce least privilege principles.

   * Monitor and audit access to sensitive data in real-time to detect and respond to any unauthorized activities or security breaches promptly.

   * Develop and enforce data retention policies to ensure compliance with regulatory

Figure 7.12: Interacting with ChatGPT

Time Management

Students can leverage time management prompts for planning their schedule, planning their time between school /college or home activity, create a project or assignment plan, prioritize and planning their task.

Here are some general inputs for time management prompts:

- Create a weekly calendar to allocate time between homework, study, extracurricular activities, and relaxation.
- Set specific goals for project completion and tracking their progress over time.
- Planning your tasks based on priorities and develop strategies for their effective management.

Here is sample prompt:

- **Prompt**: I am a student of class 6th grade. I have 8 hrs. for my school and corresponding transportation. What can be my calendar for the rest of the day for activities like homework, extracurricular activities and relaxation.

You

I am student of class 6th grade. I have 8 hrs for my school and corresponding transportation. What can be my calender for rest of the day for activities like homework, extracurricular activities and relaxation.

ChatGPT

As a 6th-grade student with 8 hours allocated for school and transportation, it's essential to have a well-balanced schedule that allows for homework, extracurricular activities, relaxation, and sufficient sleep. Here's a sample calendar for your daily activities:

6:00 AM - 7:00 AM: Wake Up and Morning Routine

- Wake up, brush teeth, and get dressed
- Eat a healthy breakfast

7:00 AM - 8:00 AM: Travel to School

- Take transportation to school

8:00 AM - 3:00 PM: School Hours

- Attend classes, participate in activities, and complete assignments

3:00 PM - 3:30 PM: Travel from School

- Return home from school

↓

3:30 PM - 4:00 PM: Relaxation Time

Figure 7.13: Interacting with ChatGPT

Communication

Students can leverage communication prompts for debates preparation, preparation for group discussion, advocating on some specific topic.

Let's have a look at some example communication prompts as below.

- **Prompt 1**: "Write an influential essay advocating for a specific cause or idea."
- **Prompt 2**: "Prepare a persuasive speech on specific topic of your choice."

Collaboration

Students can leverage collaborative prompts for participating in teamwork. This teamwork can be related to project/assignment planning within the group /class or participating in the group for problem solving activity and each team member contributes ideas or solution.

Here are some inputs while writing collaboration prompts:

- Reflect on your teamwork experience and identify areas for improvement in communication and collaboration.
- Work in teams to plan and execute a group project, assigning roles and responsibilities.

Here is a sample prompt:

- **Prompt**: I am pursuing my B.Tech, currently in my 3rd year. I am an intern. I am developing a full stack application for attendance management along with other 2 colleagues. I need to develop this application in one month using python and backend SQL database. I need to host this application on AWS cloud. Please help me create a plan for this application development considering 3 resources working on this project.

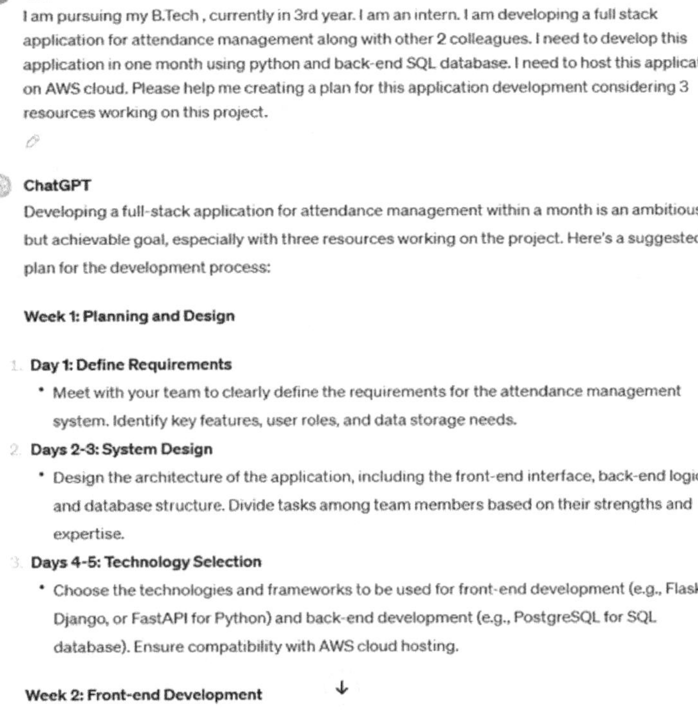

You

I am pursuing my B.Tech , currently in 3rd year. I am an intern. I am developing a full stack application for attendance management along with other 2 colleagues. I need to develop this application in one month using python and back-end SQL database. I need to host this application on AWS cloud. Please help me creating a plan for this application development considering 3 resources working on this project.

ChatGPT

Developing a full-stack application for attendance management within a month is an ambitious but achievable goal, especially with three resources working on the project. Here's a suggested plan for the development process:

Week 1: Planning and Design

1. **Day 1: Define Requirements**
   * Meet with your team to clearly define the requirements for the attendance management system. Identify key features, user roles, and data storage needs.
2. **Days 2-3: System Design**
   * Design the architecture of the application, including the front-end interface, back-end logic, and database structure. Divide tasks among team members based on their strengths and expertise.
3. **Days 4-5: Technology Selection**
   * Choose the technologies and frameworks to be used for front-end development (e.g., Flask, Django, or FastAPI for Python) and back-end development (e.g., PostgreSQL for SQL database). Ensure compatibility with AWS cloud hosting.

Week 2: Front-end Development

Figure 7.14: Interacting with ChatGPT

Self-reflection

Self-reflections prompts can be leveraged identifying strengths and areas for growth in [subject/area]. What skills do users feel confident in, and where do they think need improvement. Here are some inputs for drafting prompts

- Set personal goals for academic and personal reasons and regularly reflect on your progress.
- Seek feedback from colleagues, teachers, or mentors and use it to identify areas for growth and improvement.

Engaging Students through Creative Prompts

Prompts/prompt engineering can spark creativity and provide the engaging experience for students. Using prompts & prompt engineering, Student can actively participate in learning exercise by getting their questions clarified, which can spark their curiosity, encourage critical thinking, and promote active participation.

Here are a few examples prompts for various subjects' areas as below:

Physical Education

- Prompt 1: "Invent a new game that combines elements of favorite sports for geographic India. Describe the rules and objectives."
- Prompt 2: "Design a workout routine for 30 to 50 age group people and explain why each exercise is important for overall fitness."

Let's try ChatGPT:

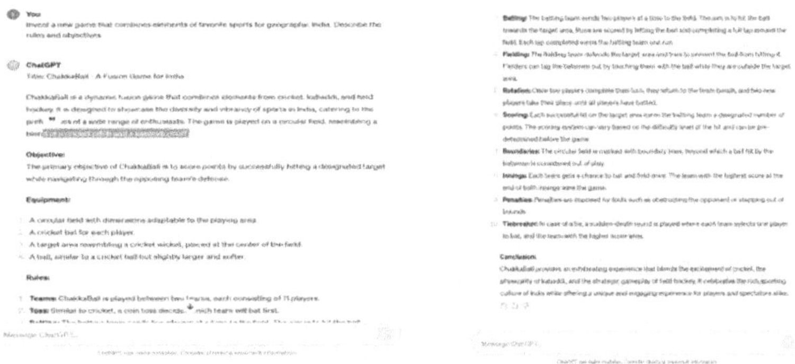

Figure 7.15: Interacting with ChatGPT

English/Language

- Prompt 1: "Compose a poem using only words found in a newspaper headline."
- Prompt 2: "Write a short story that begins with the specific sentence "

Let's try ChatGPT:

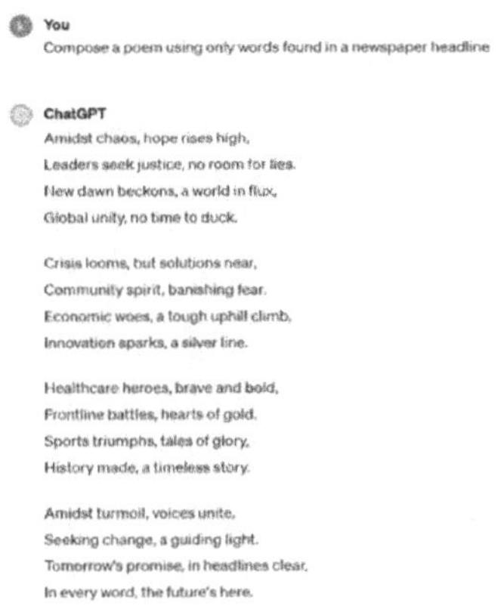

Figure 7.16: Interacting with ChatGPT

Science

- Prompt 1: "How long it will take me to reach to Sun planet".
- Prompt 2:" Design a new species that could survive in extreme environments, explaining its adaptations.

Let's try ChatGPT:

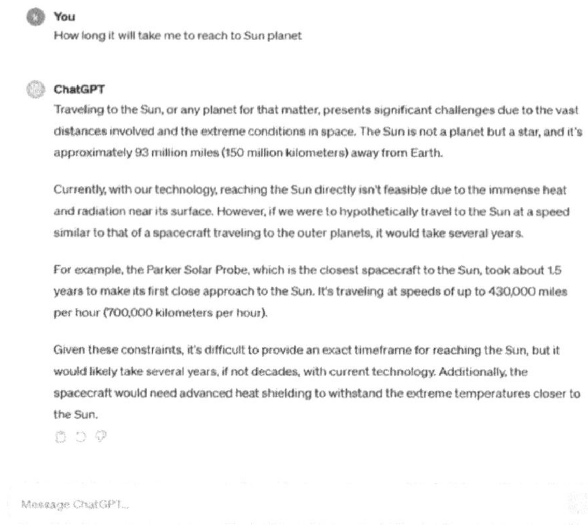

Figure 7.17: Interacting with ChatGPT

Social Studies/History

- Prompt 1: Design a board game based on a India specific historical period or events for age group 5 to 15 years and explain how players would learn about history while playing.
- Prompt 2: Study a map of the world or a specific region and identify key geographical features, landmarks, and political boundaries. Discuss the significance of these features in shaping the history, culture, and interactions of different societies throughout time.

Let's try with ChatGPT:

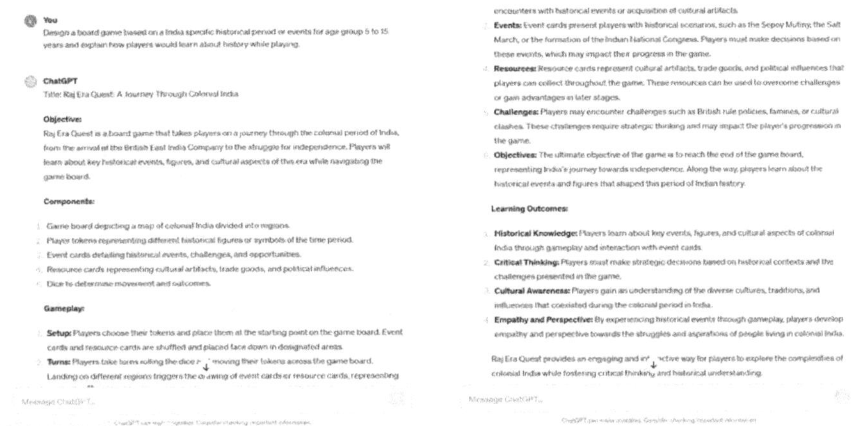

Figure 7.18: Interacting with ChatGPT

Incorporating these creative prompts in the teaching methodology, Educators can make learning more enjoyable for students as well as teachers too.

Conclusion

Prompts can play a significant role in education and training. It can help to make education/studies more interesting, creative, and engaging for both students & educator both. It can spark or ignite creative thinking and curiosity for students and teachers both. This can be helpful for various skill development aspects too. On other side, it can also help for their self-reflection that can help in growth and improvement area to identify and work further to address it.

Prompt engineering and generative AI tools and technology is going to play a transformative role in education and training for fostering engagement, innovation, critical thinking, skill development and so on in several ways as described and discussed in this chapter.

Exercise: Test Your Understanding

Answer the following questions and test your understanding of learning from Chapter 7:

Q. 1. Describe how prompts can be utilized to enhance classroom discussions. Provide an example of a prompt that could be used in a history lesson.

Q. 2. How can prompts be designed to enhance problem-solving skills in students? Give an example related to mathematics.

Q. 3. Explain the importance of creative prompts in engaging students. Provide an example of a creative writing prompt for an English class.

Q. 4. How can combining different prompts (e.g., visual, auditory, textual) create a comprehensive learning experience? Provide an example of such a combination.

Q. 5. What criteria should be used to evaluate the effectiveness of prompts in the classroom? Discuss one method for assessing student responses to prompts.

Chapter 8
Digital Tools for Prompt Engineering

So far, we have explored various techniques and methods to be good at prompt engineering and we are well equipped to use these techniques to craft prompts that generate desirable results. To help us further with writing effective prompts, we have various tools available that make our job easier.

This chapter aims to equip beginners with a comprehensive understanding of the digital tools available for practical, prompt engineering. By delving into online prompt generators, prompt management apps and integrating prompts into digital workflows, readers will gain practical insights into optimizing their use of these tools for enhanced AI model outputs.

In this chapter, we will cover:

- Online Prompt Generators
- Prompt Management Apps
- Integrating Prompts into Digital Workflows

Online Prompt Generators

As we know, coming up with an effective and useful prompt can be complex and requires perseverance and iterations which may take a good amount of time. An optimal written prompt needs thorough understanding of the model and producing the required output needs precision. We also know that simply rephrasing the prompt can also alter the generated output by the models significantly.

Thus, prompt engineering best practices include experimentation and trying different techniques to get to the best prompt.

To expedite this process and help achieve the desired prompt, there are several online prompt generators tools available that help to refine our prompts be it for writing using models like GPT, Google Bard, etc. or image generation models using Stable Diffusion, DALL·E 2 and Midjourney, etc. or any other use cases.

Thus, AI Prompt generators are tools that use natural language processing and machine learning algorithms to generate helpful prompts which serve as a beginning point for prompt creation. The prompt is generated by providing criteria like genre, tone, or any specific context.

The prompt generators not only save time but also spart creativity leading to fresh ideas. They can be used for a variety of purposes like creative writing, coding, brainstorming, in education, community and social engagements, entertainment, for research and much more.

Here are some popular online prompt generators:

Prompt Perfect

Prompt Perfect is an advanced AI-powered tool designed to refine and optimize user prompts for generating high-quality, contextually accurate responses. It leverages sophisticated algorithms to enhance clarity, precision, and relevance, ensuring that the prompts yield the most effective and insightful results.

Following are the main features of Prompt Perfect:

- Can be used to make prompts for Claude, GPT4, Lexica, Midjourney, ChatGPT, Stable Diffusion, and more
- User friendly interface to optimize prompts
- Can compare before and after prompt optimization
- Can compare outputs from various models

- Prompts can be deployed as a service and can be integrated with other tools and platform via its APIs
- Can optimize large batches of prompts in one shot
- Prompts can be optimized in multiple languages

How it works?

Prompt Perfect works by analyzing user-input prompts and applying a series of optimization techniques to enhance their effectiveness. The tool uses natural language processing (NLP) algorithms to evaluate the clarity, context, and intent of the prompt.

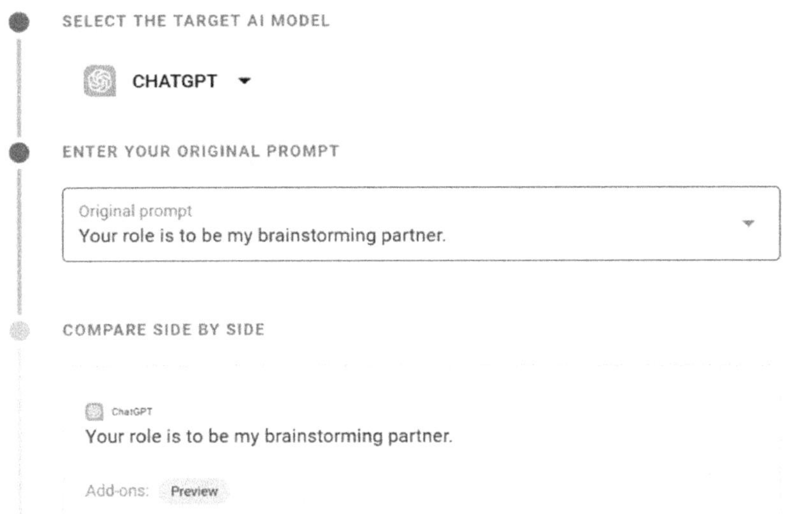

Figure 8.1: Selecting a Model

It then refines the prompt by suggesting improvements in wording, structure, and specificity. These enhancements ensure that the AI generates responses that are more accurate, relevant, and aligned with the user's objectives. Users can iteratively refine their prompts with Prompt Perfect until the desired level of quality and precision is achieved.

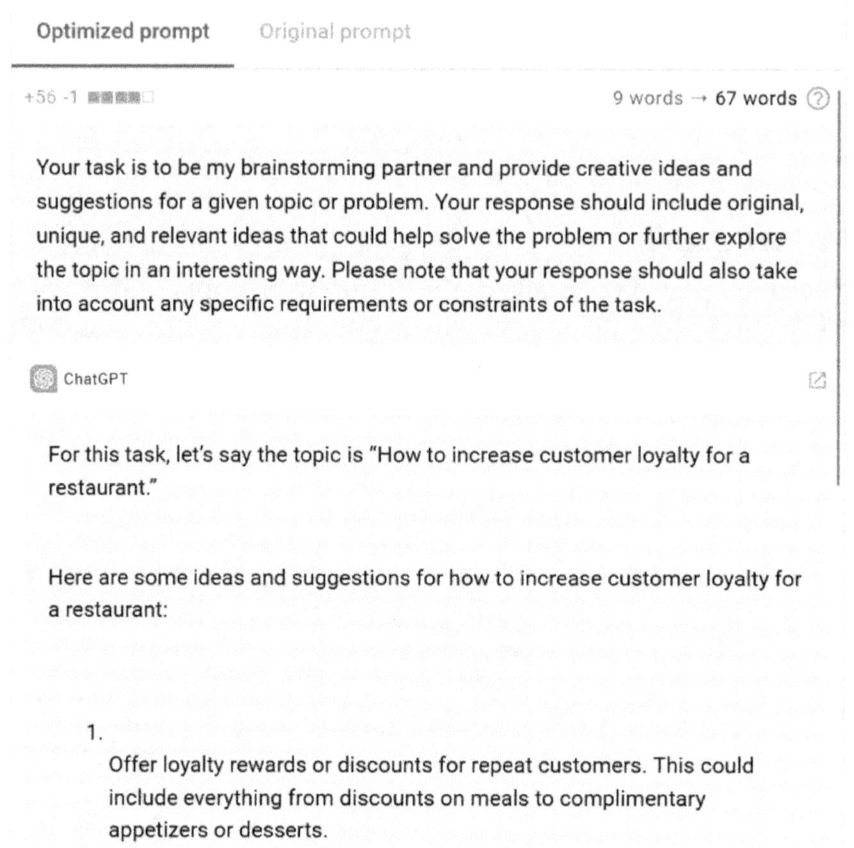

Figure 8.2: Optimizing a Prompt

As seen above, the optimized prompt generates a much more effective output
with a unique perspective rather than the original prompt would.

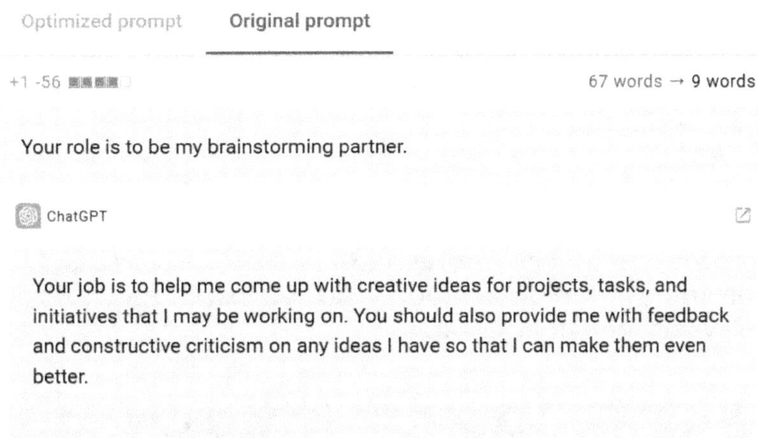

Figure 8.3: Visualizing Original Prompt

As we discussed, Prompt Perfect is a cutting-edge AI tool that refines user
prompts for superior response generation. By leveraging advanced NLP algorithms, it enhances the clarity, context, and intent of prompts, ensuring
high-quality, relevant, and precise outputs. This iterative refinement process
empowers users to achieve optimal results, making Prompt Perfect an invaluable resource for anyone seeking to harness the full potential of AI-driven interactions.

Prompt Base

Prompt base is a structured system designed to generate, manage, and refine
prompts for various applications such as education, creative writing, and skill
development. By leveraging predefined or custom prompts, users can stimulate critical thinking, creativity, and engagement in their respective fields. This
approach ensures that the prompts are relevant, effective, and tailored to the
specific needs of the audience, whether it be students, writers, or professionals seeking to enhance their skills. Overall, a prompt base serves as a valuable
tool for guiding thought processes and facilitating productive discussions and
activities.

Following are the main features of Prompt Base:

- Marketplace where users can search for and sell prompts that work with different artificial intelligence (AI) models, such as ChatGPT, DALL-E, Midjourney, and Stable Diffusion.
- Huge collection of pre-designed prompts for a very vast myriad of applica-

tions like art, poetry, creative writing, code generation, problem solving etc.
- Offers a community for prompt engineers supporting and encouraging them.
- Helps to create AI Apps using prompts as well as explore apps.
- Publishes new, featured and trending prompts with top prompts and top creators as well,

How it works?

The interface provides a very interesting view of the various categories to help explore prompts based on AI models, Art, Logos, Graphics, Productivity & Writing, etc. as visualized in `Figure 8.4`

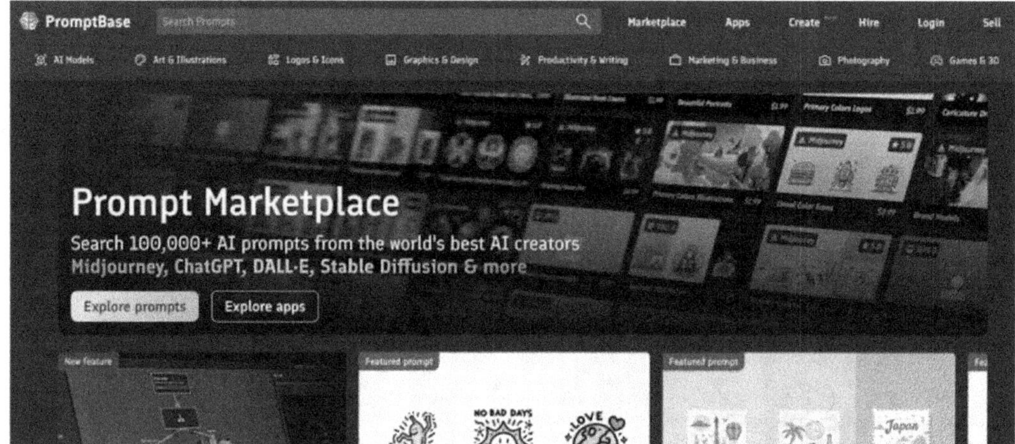

Figure 8.4: Prompt Marketplace

Let us explore one category.

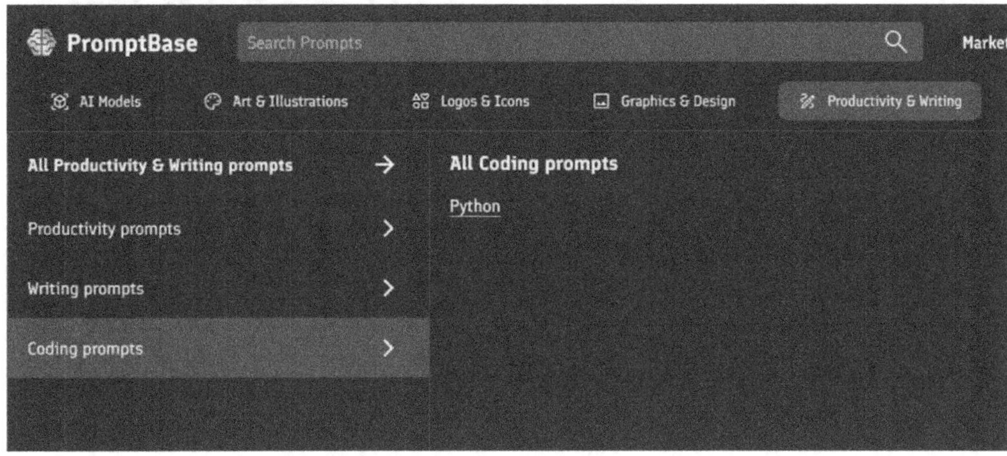

Figure 8.5: PromptBase: Coding Prompts

This gives us the top python coding prompts, the most popular ones as well as some more good ones.

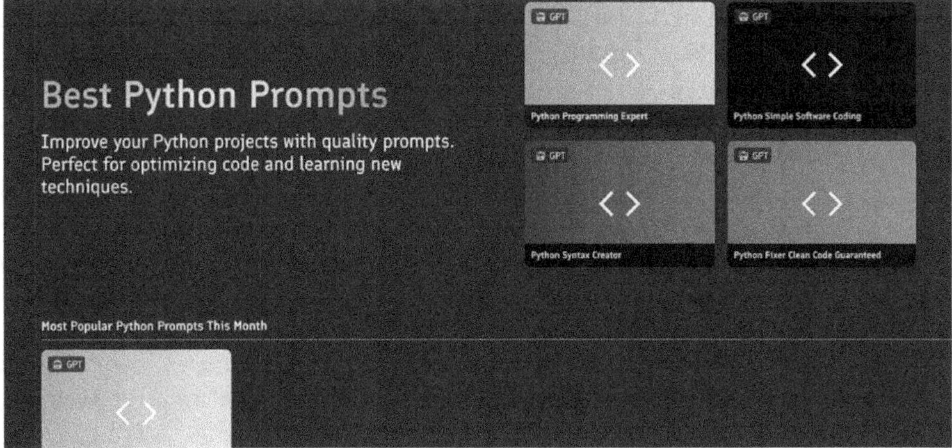

Figure 8.6: Best Python Prompts

If I explore the Python Programming Expert, I see the below which basically can be of great help to expedite or accelerate my python programming.

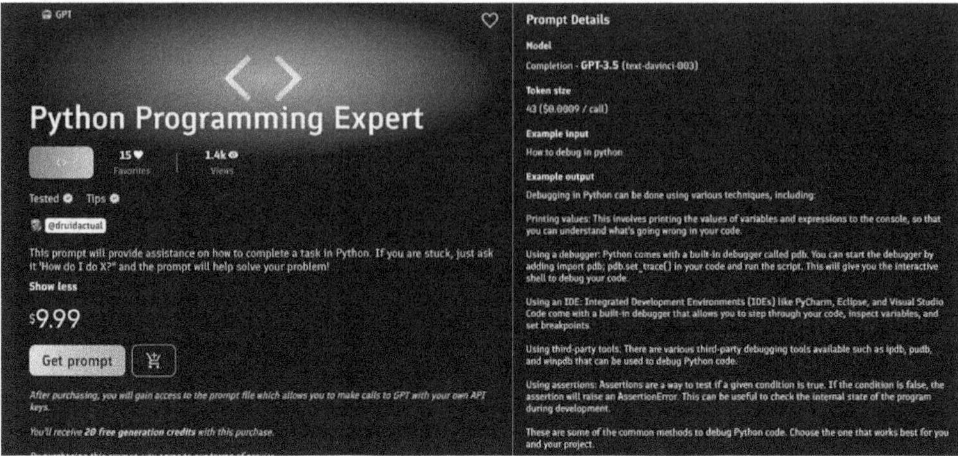

Figure 8.7: Python Programming Expert

Overall, a PromptBase serves as a valuable tool for guiding thought processes and facilitating productive discussions and activities. By offering structured and tailored prompts, it enhances engagement and stimulates creativity across various applications. Whether in education, creative writing, or skill development, a well-designed prompt base ensures that users can effectively achieve their objectives and foster meaningful interactions.

PromptHero

PromptHero is an innovative platform designed to streamline the process of prompt engineering. It provides a comprehensive suite of tools and resources for creating, managing, and optimizing prompts for various applications, including AI training and classroom activities. With intuitive interface and advanced analytics, PromptHero empowers educators, developers, and content creators to craft effective and engaging prompts that enhance learning and productivity. Additionally, the platform supports collaborative workflows, making it easier for teams to work together and achieve their prompt-related goals efficiently.

Following are the main features of PromptHero:

- The biggest prompt database for AI picture generating models, including Midjourney, DALL-E, and stable diffusion, etc
- Customizable prompts, allow you to experiment with different styles and formats
- Encourages prompt engineers to collaborate and interact as a community

- User friendly, intuitive approach to searching prompts
- Has a Prompt builder helping the prompt engineers to refine their prompts
- Publishes latest trends and techniques from experienced prompt engineers

How it works?

PromptHero works by providing a user-friendly interface where users can create, manage, and analyze prompts for their specific needs.

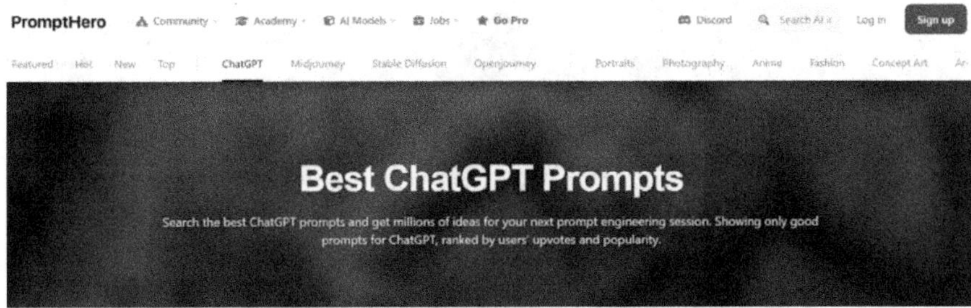

Figure 8.8: PromptHero Landing Page

Here's how it works:

- **Creation**: Users can create prompts using a variety of tools and templates tailored to their objectives. They can choose from different types of prompts, such as text-based, image-based, or audio-based, and customize them according to their requirements.
- **Management**: Once created, prompts can be organized, edited, and categorized within the platform. Users can easily search for and retrieve prompts based on keywords or tags, making it simple to reuse and repurpose prompts for different projects.
- **Optimization**: PromptHero offers analytics and feedback mechanisms to help users optimize their prompts for maximum effectiveness. Users can track metrics such as engagement rates, response times, and user feedback to refine their prompts over time.
- **Collaboration**: The platform supports collaboration, allowing multiple users to work together on creating and refining prompts. Users can share prompts, provide feedback, and collaborate in real-time to enhance the quality of their prompts.
- **Integration**: PromptHero can be integrated with other tools and platforms, such as AI models, educational software, and content management systems, to seamlessly incorporate prompts into existing workflows and applications

Clicking on any art pops up the prompt that helped to generate the art which can be edited, copied and shared.

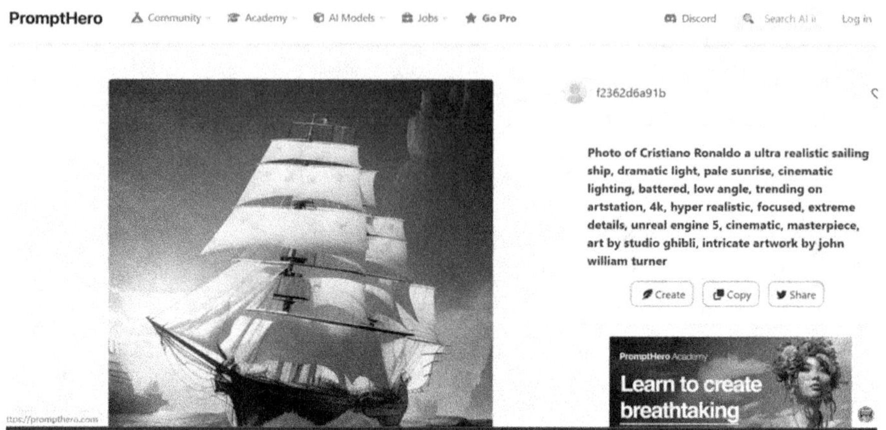

Figure 8.9: PromptHero in Action

PromptHero is a powerful platform that revolutionizes prompt engineering by providing a comprehensive set of tools and resources. Its user-friendly interface, advanced analytics, and collaborative features make it an invaluable tool for educators, developers, and content creators alike. By simplifying the process of creating, managing, and optimizing prompts, PromptHero empowers users to enhance learning, drive engagement, and achieve their prompt-related goals with ease.

Prompt Management Apps

Prompt Management is optimizing, organizing, saving and retrieving prompts as required when working with AI models.

Using effective prompt management techniques makes it easier to keep track of different versions of your prompts and continue to optimize them for usage and enhancement.

It is like maintaining a library of prompts which is well-organized.

To be able to manage prompts effectively, there are several management apps available, and we will explore some of them.

PromptBetter

PromptBetter is a unique intermediary layer that empowers AI enthusiasts to refine and enhance their AI interactions using A/B testing, real-time user feedback, and performance monitoring. Specifically designed as a plugin for open API prompt management, PromptBetter provides a streamlined approach to optimizing and transforming AI interactions for improved user engagement and effectiveness

Following are the main features of PromptBetter:

- Gives control over prompts by managing them effectively
- Helps to store and modify prompts using an accessible and easy user interface. So any member can optimise and edit prompts.
- Provides logs for each request from the user, thus providing insights into human behaviour
- Helps manage versions of your prompts by providing A/B testing
- Helps to track and record user feedback of the prompt results

PromptFolder

PromptFolder is an innovative AI tool designed to assist users in managing and organizing prompts for platforms such as ChatGPT or MidJourney. Its intuitive interface simplifies the process of creating, editing, and saving prompts for future reference, enabling users to maintain a library of prompts tailored to their needs. By providing a user-friendly solution for prompt management, PromptFolder enhances the efficiency and effectiveness of utilizing AI tools for various applications.

Following are the main features of PromptFolder:

- Seamless integration with ChatGPT
- Prompt Organization
- Private/public access control
- Library for trending prompts

ZenPrompts

ZenPrompts is a platform that offers a unique approach to creative writing prompts, focusing on mindfulness and introspection. The prompts are designed to inspire deep thinking and self-discovery, encouraging writers to explore their inner thoughts and emotions. With ZenPrompts, writers can tap into a state of calm and clarity, fostering creativity and personal growth through their writing.

Following are the main features of ZenPrompts:

- Sophisticated prompt editor
- Model comparison and selection helping you to pick the best prompt based on quality, cost and performance
- Prompt portfolios showcase by offering clean and user-friendly layouts
- Multiple version experimentation with managing and not losing any versions
- Documentation support to be able to add comments to your prompts for maintainability

ZenPrompts provides a tranquil space for writers to delve into their imagination while fostering a sense of peace and introspection. By encouraging mindful writing, ZenPrompts aims to not only inspire creativity but also promote personal reflection and growth through the art of storytelling.

Knit

Knit is a collaborative knowledge network that enables organizations to capture, organize, and share their knowledge effectively. It provides a platform for teams to create and maintain a centralized knowledge base, making information easily accessible and searchable. Knit helps improve productivity by reducing the time spent searching for information and promoting knowledge sharing within the organization.

Following are the main features of Knit:

- Centralized workspace for users to edit, save and run prompts.
- Playground mode for users to test their prompts with mocked values
- Project management for users to organize prompts and collaborate with team
- Version control to track history of saved prompts
- Security features with encryption of sensitive data while transmission and storage

There are many prompt management apps available online like PI Prompts, PromptLeo, EasyPrompt, etc.

Integrating Prompts into Digital Workflows

With the emergence of GenAI and Prompt Engineering, organizations and individuals are inquisitive about how they can adopt these new technologies in their daily tasks to raise efficiency. Adopting new tools, however, is never easy but we need to have a mindset of replacing the mundane tasks with automation through prompt engineering.

Candidates for integrating prompts into the Digital Workflows are any tasks that we do which can be enhanced or expedited by using the AI models. These workflows could range from anything like ideation to content creation to project planning or technical tasks of design, code, etc.

Some use cases for this integration could include:

Idea Generation for new Opportunities/Project

Brainstorming ideas with the team is a very effective way of finding new opportunities or potential projects. Prompts to trigger an idea can be a great starting point to give direction to the thought process.

You

You are an experienced product owner at a bank. It is time for you to choose a few places to look for projects to help bank to achieve better NPS scores. Create a list of 3 places that might be good opportunities for projects to be created and who would likely be the best contact to reach out to discuss.

ChatGPT

Certainly! Improving Net Promoter Score (NPS) involves enhancing customer experience, addressing pain points, and introducing innovative solutions. Here are three potential areas to explore for projects:

1. **Digital Banking Platform:**
   - **Opportunity:** Enhance the digital banking platform to make it more user-friendly, efficient, and feature-rich.
   - **Contact:** The Chief Technology Officer ↓ O) or Head of Digital Banking would be the key contact to discuss improvements and innovations in the digital banking space.

Figure 8.10: Interacting with ChatGPT

The above prompt helps to give a strategic direction to thoughts and the team can then start brainstorming from here onwards.

Code Builder and Quality

Integrating prompts into digital workflows involves using automated tools, often referred to as code builders, to generate code based on specific prompts or requirements. These tools can streamline the development process by quickly producing code snippets or even entire modules, saving developers time and effort. However, the quality of the generated code is crucial, as poorly written code can lead to bugs, security vulnerabilities, and maintenance issues. Therefore, it's essential to ensure that code builders produce high-quality, well-structured code that meets coding standards and best practices. This integration can significantly improve productivity and code consistency across projects when implemented correctly.

Figure 8.11: Code-snippet generation

The above prompt helps to generate a code snippet for a typical account opening scenario which can then be enhanced with the additional features, validations, etc. We can also craft prompts to debug the code, enforce coding standards, reduce vulnerabilities, create documentation, have performance improvement suggestions, and write test cases. Prompts can also be integrated into developer IDEs in their workspaces to provide real-time feedback during coding.

Chatbot Development

With Prompt engineering, we can develop and train the chatbot to handle various inputs and produce reasonable responses. The prompts can help to direct the models behavior like target audience, tone, response length and context. These models (LLMs) can be trained and fine-tuned by using different techniques that we learnt like one-shot and few-shot examples.

Example- OpenAI's GPT-3 has been trained on a 175-billion-parameter model that can generate text and computer code with short written prompts.

Organizations such as healthcare, financial services, and legal professions are adopting LLM-based chatbots for a wide range of applications.

Thus, prompt engineering becomes critical to train the chatbots in specific areas and domains by providing data specific to the field to be able to produce more relevant responses.

The chatbot can be trained to handle ambiguity, response tone, recognize user preferences, domain specific responses and also to handle sensitive information.

Content Creation

As we have explored content creation and how prompt engineering can help in creative writing in detail, we are aware of this use case. We have seen that prompt engineering can trigger creative thoughts, optimize content, set the tone and style , provide feedback to the content developer and thus help to create engaging content.

A business owner to automate their workflow and improve efficiency

For a business owner, prompt engineering can help by automating repetitive tasks or routine workflows. Prompts can also help in identifying these areas of automation. Since AI models have different capabilities, it's important for a business owner to recognize the strengths of these AI models and try to figure out which workflow they can be integrated in. Prompts can also be developed to improve data quality in business and to guide integration with other systems. We can also craft prompts to provide checks to comply with security standards and regulations. Documentation for a product or service, cost benefit analysis and producing dashboards for regular monitoring of the business can be easily integrated through prompt engineering to help.

Service Ticket Resolutions

Prompt Engineering can be of great help in the Service ticket resolution workflow as we can automate many tasks like identifying common ticket categories, gathering information, resolution steps and even write prompts to triage tickets to the right teams.

Prompts can also be written to guide agents/operations team to assess the issues, provide resolutions based on history, escalate to apt teams and to craft clear communications to customers and product owners.

Some potential steps in this workflow can also be automated through prompts like collecting feedback from customers, analyzing customer satisfaction through sentiment analysis, training support agents and implementing resolution steps that can be automated.

Enhancing Data Workflows

Integrating prompts into data workflows can greatly reduce the time and effort.

 Prompts can be written for automated data ingestion from various sources, data extraction and transformation by Natural Language Processing, Predictive modelling and scheduling algorithms.

Prompt engineering therefore enhances efficiency in data processing, analytics, and decision-making, leading to more effective data engineering processes.

Conclusion

This chapter discussed various aspects of integrating prompts into digital workflows, starting with using online prompt generators to stimulate creativity and idea generation. We then examined the role of prompt management apps in organizing and storing prompts for easy access. Finally, we delved into integrating prompts into digital workflows, highlighting the use of code builders and the importance of code quality in automated code generation. By leveraging these tools and techniques, individuals and organizations can enhance their creative processes, improve productivity, and streamline their digital workflows.

As we close this chapter, it's essential to recognize that this is just the beginning of your journey toward becoming an expert in Prompt Engineering. Thus far, you've gained a foundational understanding of Prompt Engineering, learning its basics and exploring various applications. Looking ahead, a valuable next step is creating case studies demonstrating real-world applications of Prompt Engineering. These case studies will deepen your understanding and showcase how Prompt Engineering can be effectively applied in diverse scenarios. Engaging in this practice will further enhance your skills and knowledge, paving the way for more advanced exploration and mastery of this innovative field.

Exercise: Test Your Understanding

Answer the following questions and test your understanding of learning from Chapter 8:

Q. 1. How can online prompt generators benefit writers and creatives?

Q. 2. What features should an excellent prompt management app have?

Q. 3. How can prompts be integrated into digital workflows to enhance productivity?

Q. 4. An example of how an author can use an online prompt generator to overcome a creative block.

Q. 5. How can prompt management apps improve collaboration among team members?

JOIN US ON THE
ARCCHIE PUBLICATIONS
DISCORD SERVER

Connect with fellow readers, authors, and enthusiasts to discuss all things related to our publications and the exciting world of AI, programming, and learning. Share your insights, ask questions, and engage in vibrant discussions to expand your knowledge and inspire creativity. Take advantage of this opportunity to be part of a dynamic community dedicated to exploring the frontiers of technology and innovation. Join our Discord Server today and be part of the ARCCHIE Publications community!

https://discord.gg/z26SenmpEt

Appendix-A

Answers - Test your understanding

CHAPTER 1

Answers to test your understanding, **Chapter 1**

Ans.1. The prompt is a short message or signal that tells someone what to do. Prompts are used to ask for a response or action; conversely, when you prompt someone, you're nudging or encouraging them to do something or give a specific answer. Prompt engineering is a field that helps to design and develop the best prompts to efficiently use the power of large language models (like ChatGPT) and able to generate more relevant and accurate responses.

Ans.2. Large Language model (LLM) / Prompt engineering use cases are:

1. Text generation

2. Text summarization

3. Text classification

4. Entity extraction

5. Questions and answering

6. Sentiment analysis

7. Code generation and explanation

8. Language Translation

Ans.3. The benefits of creative prompts are below:

1. Unlocking Imagination

2. Enhancing Learning

3. Boost Innovations and discoveries

4. Personal Growth

5. Problem solving

6. Media /Content Generation

7. Storytelling and poem creations

8. And many more actually.

Ans.4. Psychological principles/factors of any cognition are below, which help to improve the processing and generation of relevant responses.

1. Attentions and facts

2. Memory and retrieval cues

3. Schema activation and knowledge representation

4. Framing effects for cognitive biases

5. Motivation and goal-orientated behavior.

CHAPTER 2

Answers to test your understanding, **Chapter 2**

Ans.1. A) Write Clear instructions B) Provide Context C) Format the Prompt D) Provide Examples E) Provide Balanced Prompts F) Keep practicing.

Ans.2. Context is the background information the model retains while in the same prompting session.

Ans.3. Zero Shot Prompting technique is prompting without giving examples and relying completely on the model's pretrained knowledge.

Ans.4. Few-Shots Prompting technique is prompting with examples so that the desired output is close the examples and format provided.

Ans.5. temperature" config determines how creative or specific the response from the model can be.

CHAPTER 3

Answers to test your understanding, **Chapter 3**

Ans.1. Divergent thinking is a method for generating creative ideas by exploring many possible solutions. It can be applied using prompts to brainstorm a wide range of ideas without initially worrying about their feasibility.

Ans.2. SCAMPER is an acronym for Substitute, Combine, Adapt, Modify, Put to another use, Eliminate, and Reverse. It involves asking questions related to each component to explore new possibilities, such as modifying a coffee maker to include a timer for brewing coffee automatically.

Ans.3. Prompts provide a structured starting point that can redirect focus from mental barriers to creative possibilities. They encourage exploration and experimentation, which helps overcome constraints like fear of failure and perfectionism.

Ans.4. Expanding on a prompt-generated idea involves deepening the initial concept by asking questions like "Why?" "How?" and "What if?" It also includes combining ideas, prototyping, testing, and iteratively refining the concept based on feedback and new insights.

Ans.5. Embracing imperfection is essential because it reduces the pressure to be perfect and encourages creativity. It allows for generating a broad range of ideas, which can later be refined and developed into practical solutions.

CHAPTER 4

Answers to test your understanding, **Chapter 4**

Ans.1. Common signs of a creative block include a lack of inspiration, difficulty starting or completing projects, repetitive or unoriginal ideas, and feelings of frustration or self-doubt. To identify these in your work, observe if you are experiencing prolonged periods of inactivity, if your ideas feel stale or uninspired, if you find it challenging to make decisions, or if you frequently feel overwhelmed or discouraged about your creative projects.

Ans.2. Conventional methods for overcoming writer's block include:

- Setting a regular writing schedule.

- Creating a conducive environment.

- Breaking the work into smaller tasks.

- Free writing.

- Using writing prompts.

Techniques such as taking breaks, changing the writing location, engaging in different creative activities, and seeking peer feedback can also help. Additionally, maintaining a journal, reading widely, and setting realistic goals are effective ways to overcome writer's block.

Ans.3. AI and prompt techniques can empower you to overcome creative blocks. They provide new and diverse ideas, generate writing prompts, offer instant feedback, and suggest alternative ways to approach a topic. AI tools can analyze your writing style and propose improvements, help you brainstorm, and even automate routine tasks to free up mental space for creativity. These tools can break the monotony and stimulate creative thinking by introducing novel concepts and perspectives.

Ans.4. Strategies to navigate through an artist's block include experimenting with different mediums, taking inspiration from other artists, changing the subject matter, practicing daily sketching or doodling, and setting specific goals or challenges. Unlike writer's block, overcoming artist's block often involves more visual and tactile approaches, such as visiting galleries, collaborating with other artists, and immersing oneself in different environments to find new inspiration. Techniques like mindful observation, mood boards, and recreating classic artworks in a new style can also be effective.

Ans.5. Prompt pages are a game-changer when it comes to overcoming creative blocks. They provide a structured yet flexible starting point for your creativity, encouraging you to think outside the box and explore new ideas. These prompts can be in the form of open-ended questions, thematic inspirations, visual stimuli, or scenario-based challenges. For example, you might be prompted to 'Describe a day in the life of a fantastical creature,' 'Create a work of art that captures the essence of your favorite song,' 'Write a story that begins with a character receiving an unexpected letter,' or 'Draw a landscape from a dream you had that transports you to another world.' The key is to choose prompts that challenge you to think differently and push the boundaries of your creativity.

CHAPTER 5

Answers to test your understanding, `Chapter 5`

`Ans.1.` Prompt engineering is a powerful tool that can generate specific and thought-provoking prompts tailored to your unique writing needs. Whether you're a fiction writer, in need of detailed character scenarios, plot twists, or unique settings, or a non-fiction writer, seeking prompts that focus on personal experiences, factual events, or analytical perspectives, prompt engineering can cater to your specific requirements. This personalized approach makes prompt engineering an effective solution for overcoming writer's block and stimulating creative thinking.

`Ans.2.` Prompt engineering can suggest realistic dialogue based on character profiles, ensuring conversations sound natural and fit each character's personality. It can also provide prompts that explore character backstories, motivations, and conflicts, which deepen character development. For instance, a prompt might ask, "What is your character's greatest fear, and how does it influence their actions?" This encourages writers to think deeply about their characters.

`Ans.3.` Prompt-driven storytelling techniques can help structure a narrative by providing a framework or sequence of prompts that guide the story from beginning to end. These prompts might include setting up the scene, developing the climax, and resolving conflicts. These prompts ensure the narrative stays coherent and engaging while allowing creative flexibility.

`Ans.4.` Prompt engineering can help writers find the right balance between description and exposition by offering prompts focusing on sensory details and factual information. For example, a prompt might ask, "Describe the scene in detail, including what you see, hear, and smell," followed by another prompt that asks, "Explain the significance of this event in historical context." This approach ensures that non-fiction writing is both informative and vivid.

`Ans.5.` Common challenges include overly vague, restrictive, or uninspiring prompts. Prompt engineering can address these issues by generating clear, flexible prompts tailored to the writer's specific needs and interests. Using AI to analyze a writer's style and preferences, prompt engineering can create prompts that are more likely to resonate and inspire creativity, helping writers overcome obstacles and maintain momentum in their writing projects.

CHAPTER 6

Answers to test your understanding, **Chapter 6**

Ans.1. Do this exercise by yourself.

Ans.2. Do this exercise by yourself.

Ans.3. Do this exercise by yourself.

Ans.4. Visual prompts provide a starting point and direction, making it easier to begin the creative process. They stimulate ideas and offer inspiration, helping to overcome creative blocks by giving artists something to build on.

Ans.5. Techniques include using colors that evoke specific emotions, incorporating textures that convey feelings, and employing shapes and lines that represent different moods. For example, warm colors like red and orange evoke passion, while smooth, flowing lines convey calmness.

Ans.6. Breaking down the elements helps artists understand the core aspects of the image, such as composition, color, and mood. This understanding allows them to reconstruct these elements in their artwork, ensuring that the essence of the prompt is captured effectively.

Ans.7. Experimenting with different styles allows artists to discover new techniques and perspectives. It broadens their creative horizons and helps them find unique ways to interpret prompts, ultimately enhancing their artistic skills.

Ans.8. A storyboard helps organize the sequence of images and ensures a logical narrative flow. It allows artists to plan the composition and details of each frame, making the storytelling process more structured and coherent.

CHAPTER 7

Answers to test your understanding, **Chapter 7**

Ans.1. The strategic use of prompts in classroom discussions is a powerful tool to stimulate critical thinking, elicit diverse perspectives, and actively engage students. By posing open-ended questions or presenting scenarios, teachers can ignite students' curiosity and foster a deeper understanding of the subject. For instance, in a literature class, a prompt could be: 'What do you think the author's intention was in this passage?' In a science class, a prompt could be: 'How would you design an experiment to test this hypothesis?'

Example Prompt for a History Lesson: *"Imagine you are a citizen in Ancient Rome. How would you feel about the changes brought by the Roman Empire's expansion? Discuss the positive and negative impacts on your daily life."*.

Ans.2. When it comes to problem-solving, prompts play a crucial role. They are designed to challenge students to think critically and explore various solutions. These prompts should encourage analytical thinking, reasoning, and the application of concepts to real-world scenarios, preparing students for practical challenges they may face in the future. To design effective prompts, consider the learning objectives, the complexity of the problem, and the student's prior knowledge and skills. A well-designed prompt should be clear, concise, and thought-provoking.

Example Prompt for Mathematics: In this budgeting exercise, we aim to develop students' financial literacy and decision-making skills. The prompt is as follows: *"You have a budget of $100 to buy school supplies for the year. List the items you would purchase and calculate the total cost. Ensure you stay within the budget and justify your choices based on their necessity."*.

Ans.3. Creative prompts are not just crucial in engaging students, they also inspire educators. They ignite imagination, inspire original thinking, and make learning enjoyable. They help students express themselves, explore new ideas, and develop a love for learning, sparking inspiration in educators as well.

Example Creative Writing Prompt for English Class: *"Write a short story about a world where people communicate only through music. How would everyday interactions change? Describe a day in the life of a character living in this world."*.

Ans.4. The adaptability of different types of prompts can cater to diverse learning styles, making the learning experience more immersive and engaging. Visual prompts can enhance understanding, auditory prompts can improve listening skills, and textual prompts can strengthen reading and writing abilities, giving educators the confidence to meet diverse student needs.

Example Combination: For a science lesson on ecosystems, we can use a visual prompt like a diagram of a food web to enhance understanding, an auditory prompt such as a recording of different animal sounds to improve listening skills, and a textual prompt asking students to write a paragraph explaining the interdependence of species within the ecosystem to strengthen reading and writing abilities.

Ans.5. The effectiveness of prompts can be evaluated based on criteria such as student engagement, the depth of responses, critical thinking demonstrated, and the relevance to learning objectives. One method for assessing student responses is using rubrics, which outline specific expectations and provide clear benchmarks for performance levels. For instance, a rubric might include categories such as 'comprehension of the prompt ', 'depth of analysis ', and 'clarity of expression '.

CHAPTER 8

Answers to test your understanding, `Chapter 8`

Ans.1. Online prompt generators provide a quick and easy way to overcome writer's block, spark creativity, and explore new ideas. They offer prompts across different genres and styles, catering to diverse interests and preferences.

Ans.2. A good prompt management app should be able to organize prompts into categories or themes, allow users to create custom prompts, provide options for scheduling and reminders, and offer a user-friendly interface for easy access and navigation.

Ans.3. Prompts can be integrated into digital workflows through tools like task management apps, calendar apps, and writing software. Setting up prompts for specific tasks or goals allows users to stay focused, manage their time effectively, and achieve better results.

Ans.4. An author struggling to develop ideas for their next novel can generate a random plot twist using an online prompt generator. This unexpected twist can inspire new directions for the story and help break through the creative block.

Ans.5. Prompt management apps can improve collaboration by allowing team members to share and discuss prompts, provide feedback, and track progress on shared projects. They can also help ensure that everyone is aligned with the project goals and deadlines.

Appendix-B

Exercise – Do It Yourself

EXERCISE: EXPLORING VISUAL PROMPTS IN ILLUSTRATION AND ART

Take a simple visual prompt, like a photograph of a bustling city street, and create three different illustrations based on it: one realistic, one abstract, and one surreal.

In this exercise, we will take a single visual prompt and explore how it can inspire different styles of illustration. By creating three distinct pieces based on the same visual prompt—a photograph of a bustling city street—, you will practice shifting your perspective and approach to see how varied artistic interpretations can be. This exercise will help you understand how to adapt a visual prompt to suit different artistic goals and styles.

Visual Prompt: Photograph of a Bustling City Street

Imagine a photograph showing a busy city street filled with people, vehicles, buildings, and various activities. The scene is vibrant with colors, movement, and a mix of modern and historical architecture.

Objective: Create three different illustrations based on the given visual prompt:

- A realistic illustration
- An abstract illustration
- A surreal illustration

Part 1: Realistic Illustration

A realistic illustration aims to capture the scene as it appears in real life, with attention to detail and accurate representation of the elements.

Observation and Analysis
- Carefully examine the photograph. Note the details such as the people's clothing, the types of vehicles, architectural styles, and the overall atmosphere.
- Pay attention to light and shadows, the colors, and the textures in the scene.

Sketching the Scene
- Start with a rough sketch to lay out the composition. Focus on the main elements: buildings, streets, people, and vehicles.
- Gradually add details, refining the shapes and lines to match the photograph.

Adding Color and Texture
- Use a color palette that matches the photograph. Pay attention to the different hues and tones.
- Add textures to give buildings, streets, and other elements a realistic feel. Consider using techniques like hatching, stippling, or smooth shading.

Final Touches
- Add final details such as shadows, reflections, and highlights to enhance the realism.
- Review the illustration to ensure it accurately reflects the bustling city street in the photograph.

Part 2: Abstract Illustration

An abstract illustration takes the scene's essence and expresses it through shapes, colors, and forms without focusing on realistic representation.

Extracting the Essence

- Identify the core elements and emotions of the city street scene. This could be the sense of movement, the contrast of colors, or the overall energy.

Simplifying and Distorting

- Simplify the elements into basic shapes and forms. Buildings may become rectangles; lines or curves represent people and vehicles by geometric shapes.
- Experiment with distorting these shapes to convey motion and energy.

Color and Composition

- Choose a color scheme that represents the mood of the scene. Bright, contrasting colors convey vibrancy, while muted tones suggest a more subdued atmosphere.
- Arrange the shapes and colors to balance the composition and guide the viewer's eye through the artwork.

Expressive Techniques

- Use splattering, blending, or layering techniques to add depth and interest.
- Focus on creating a piece that evokes the feeling of a bustling city street rather than a literal depiction.

Part 3: Surreal Illustration

A surreal illustration blends reality with imagination, creating a fantastical version of the city street that defies logical rules and evokes a dreamlike quality.

Imaginative Elements

- Introduce fantastical elements to the scene. Buildings could be floating, people might have unusual features, or vehicles could transform into strange creatures.
- Think about how the elements of the city street can be exaggerated or altered to create a surreal effect.

Sketching the Unusual

- Start with a basic layout of the scene, incorporating both realistic and imaginative elements.
- Play with scale, perspective, and composition to enhance the surreal quality. For example, a tiny person might be walking next to a giant floating building.

Color and Light

- Use colors that enhance the surreal atmosphere. This might include unexpected color combinations or using colors to highlight the fantastical

elements.
- Manipulate light and shadow to create a sense of depth and mystery.

Detailing the Surreal

- Add intricate details to both the realistic and imaginative parts of the illustration. This contrast can enhance the surreal effect.
- Include elements that challenge reality, such as melting structures, floating objects, or whimsical creatures interacting with the environment.

Reflecting on the Exercise

After completing the three illustrations, take some time to reflect on the process:

- Compare and Contrast: Look at the three pieces side by side. How does each style change the interpretation of the same visual prompt?
- Challenges and Discoveries: What challenges did you face in each style? What new techniques or approaches did you discover?
- Personal Preferences: Which style did you enjoy the most? How might you incorporate these techniques into your future work?

This exercise demonstrates the versatility of visual prompts and how they can inspire a wide range of artistic expressions. By practicing different styles, you can expand your creative toolkit and develop a more flexible and imaginative approach to your art.

EXERCISE: CREATING ABSTRACT ARTWORK USING A VISUAL PROMPT

Create an abstract artwork using a visual prompt like a stormy sea. Focus on conveying the energy and chaos of the storm through your choice of colors and brushstrokes.

To proceed with this exercise, you need the following materials:

- Canvas or paper
- Acrylic or oil paints (or any preferred medium)
- Brushes of various sizes
- Palette knives (optional)
- Visual prompt: An image of a stormy sea

The followings are the steps to complete this exercise:

Step 1: Analyze the Visual Prompt

Begin by examining the visual prompt – an image of a stormy sea. Notice the elements that stand out to you:

- The swirling, turbulent waves
- The dark, ominous clouds
- The contrast between the frothy whitecaps and the deep, dark water
- The sense of movement and chaos

Step 2: Choose Your Color Palette

Select colors that will help convey the mood and energy of the stormy sea. Consider using:

- Deep blues and greens for the water
- Dark grays and blacks for the storm clouds
- Bright whites and lighter blues for the wave crests and foam
- Accents of purple or indigo add depth and intensity

Step 3: Plan Your Composition

Think about how you want to arrange the elements on your canvas. An abstract artwork doesn't need to represent reality directly but should capture the scene's essence. Consider:

- Using sweeping, swirling lines to represent the movement of the waves
- Placing areas of intense color and contrast to highlight the storm's power

- Creating a sense of depth by layering different shades and textures

Step 4: Start with Broad Strokes

Embark on your artistic journey by embracing the chaos of the stormy sea. Begin with broad, sweeping brushstrokes to lay down the base colors, setting the stage for the overall movement and energy of the piece. At this stage, details are not a concern; the focus is on capturing the general flow and chaos of the stormy sea. This is where the adventure and anticipation of your artwork start to unfold.

Tips:

- Use a large brush or palette knife to apply paint quickly and boldly.
- Let the colors blend on the canvas to create natural transitions and a sense of movement.
- Experiment with different angles and directions for your brushstrokes to mimic the unpredictable nature of a storm.

Step 5: Add Layers and Details

Once you have the base layer, add more layers to build depth and complexity. Use smaller brushes to add details and highlights, such as:

- Lighter colors for the wave crests and foam
- Darker shades create shadows and depth in the water and clouds
- Accents of different colors add interest and texture

Tips:

- Apply paint in varying thicknesses to create texture and contrast.
- Use short, quick strokes to represent the choppy water.
- Blend and smooth certain areas to depict the swirling motion of the storm.

Step 6: Focus on the Emotion

As you add layers and details, keep focusing on the emotional impact of your artwork. The goal is to convey the energy and chaos of the storm, so don't be afraid to let your brushstrokes be expressive and dynamic. Think about how the stormy sea makes you feel – anxious, awe-struck, overwhelmed – and try to capture those emotions in your painting.

Step 7: Step Back and Evaluate

Periodically step back from your artwork to see it from a distance. This will help you assess the overall composition and ensure that the energy and movement are effectively conveyed. Look for areas that need more contrast, color, or texture to enhance the sense of chaos and power.

Step 8: Refine and Finish

Once satisfied with the overall composition and emotional impact, add any final touches to refine your painting.

This might include:

- Adding highlights to areas that need more emphasis
- Smoothing or blending certain sections for better flow
- Intensifying colors or shadows to enhance contrast

Step 9: Reflect and Review

After completing your artwork, take some time to reflect on the process and the final piece. Consider:

- What techniques were most effective in conveying the energy and chaos of the stormy sea?
- How did the use of color and brushstrokes impact the emotional tone of the artwork?
- What did you learn about using visual prompts to create abstract art?

This exercise helps you explore how visual prompts can inspire abstract art. By focusing on conveying the energy and chaos of a stormy sea through your choice of colors and brushstrokes, you can develop a deeper understanding of how to translate abstract concepts into visual forms. Remember, the goal is not to replicate the prompt image precisely but to capture its essence and emotional impact through your unique artistic expression.

EXERCISE: CREATING VISUAL NARRATIVES WITH PROMPTS

Choose a visual prompt, like a photograph of a carnival, and create a short comic strip that tells a story based on that image. Focus on developing characters and a plot that fits the prompt.

In this exercise, you'll choose a visual prompt and use it as the basis for creating a short comic strip. This will help you practice developing characters and plots that fit the chosen prompt, enhancing your skills in visual storytelling.

Step 1: Choose a Visual Prompt

First, immerse yourself in the world of curiosity and select a visual prompt that truly captivates you. For this exercise, let's use a photograph of a carnival. Envision a vibrant scene with lively performers, colorful tents, and visitors brimming with excitement. What mysteries might be concealed within this seemingly ordinary carnival?

Step 2: Analyze the Visual Prompt

Take a few moments to study the photograph closely. Observe the details, such as the various carnival attractions, the people in the scene, and the overall atmosphere. Consider the following questions:

- What elements stand out to you?
- What kind of emotions does the image evoke?
- What stories could be happening in this setting?

Step 3: Develop Characters

Based on the visual prompt, create a set of characters who will be part of your comic strip. Here are some character ideas:

- **The Young Adventurer**: A curious child eager to explore every corner of the carnival.
- **The Mysterious Performer**: An enigmatic magician who captivates the audience with their tricks.
- **The Friendly Vendor**: A cheerful person running a cotton candy stand interacting with visitors.
- **The Mischievous Pet**: A playful dog that gets into trouble, adding humor to the story.

Step 4: Outline the Plot

Next, outline a simple plot for your comic strip. Keep it concise, as the goal is to create a short, engaging story. Here's a possible plot outline:

- **Introduction**: The young adventurer arrives at the carnival wide-eyed and excited.
- **Rising Action**: The adventurer meets the mysterious performer, who offers to show a unique trick.
- **Climax**: The trick goes awry, causing humorous events involving the friendly vendor and the mischievous pet.
- **Falling Action**: The chaos is resolved, and everyone shares a laugh.
- **Conclusion**: The adventurer leaves the carnival with fond memories and a newfound friend in the performer.

Step 5: Create a Script

Write a script for your comic strip, including dialogue and descriptions of each panel. The script should guide the reader through the story, describing the actions and dialogue of each character. Here's a script example based on the outline:

Panel 1: Introduction

- **Image**: The young adventurer enters the carnival, eyes wide with wonder.
- **Dialogue**: (Adventurer) "Wow! Look at all the amazing attractions!"

Panel 2: Rising Action

- **Image**: The adventurer approaches the mysterious performer, surrounded by a small crowd.
- **Dialogue**: (Performer) "Step right up, young one! How about a magic trick?"

Panel 3: Climax

- **Image**: The performer waves a wand, but the trick goes wrong, causing the mischievous pet to steal a hat from the vendor.
- **Dialogue**: (Vendor) "Hey, get back here with my hat!"

Panel 4: Falling Action

- Image: The adventurer helps the performer and vendor chase the pet, leading to a funny sequence.
- Dialogue: (Adventurer) "I've got it! Oh no, it slipped away again!"

Panel 5: Conclusion

- Image: The adventurer, performer, vendor, and pet are all smiling, and the hat

is returned to its owner.
- Dialogue: (Performer) "Thanks for the help, kid. That was quite an adventure!"

Step 6: Draw the Comic Strip

Now, it's time to bring your story to life visually. Create the comic strip by drawing each panel based on the script. Focus on clearly depicting the characters, actions, and emotions. If you need more confidence in your drawing skills, simple sketches will do; the key is effectively conveying the story. Consider the layout of each panel, the placement of characters and objects, and the use of colors and shading to enhance the mood and atmosphere of the scene. Remember, the visuals are just as important as the story in a comic strip, so take your time and enjoy the process of drawing. If you're not sure how to draw a certain element, consider looking up tutorials or practicing specific drawing techniques to improve your skills.

Step 7: Review and Refine

After completing your comic strip, it's important to review it to ensure the story flows smoothly and the visuals align with the script. This is your opportunity to make any necessary adjustments to improve clarity and impact. If you're looking for more guidance or inspiration, consider checking out online tutorials, books on comic creation, or joining a community of comic creators. These resources can provide valuable insights and feedback to help you improve your storytelling and drawing skills. Remember, the more you practice and refine your work, the better your comic strips will become.

Example Comic Strip

Panel 1

- Image: The carnival entrance with the young adventurer looking amazed.
- Text: "Wow! Look at all the amazing attractions!"

Panel 2

- Image: The performer in a colorful costume, surrounded by a small audience.
- Text: "Step right up, young one! How about a magic trick?"

Panel 3

- Image: The pet grabs the vendor's hat, causing chaos.
- Text: "Hey, get back here with my hat!"

Panel 4

- Image: The chase scene shows the adventurer, performer, and vendor running after the pet.

- Text: "I've got it! Oh no, it slipped away again!"

Panel 5

- Image: All characters smiling, with the hat returned.
- Text: "Thanks for the help, kid. That was quite an adventure!"

Reflection and Learning

Take some time to reflect on the exercise. Consider the following questions:

- How did the visual prompting influence your story?
- What challenges did you encounter while developing the plot and characters?
- How did the exercise help you improve your visual storytelling skills?

By completing this exercise, you've practiced using visual prompts to create a narrative, developed your ability to translate abstract ideas into a coherent story, and enhanced your understanding of character and plot development in visual storytelling.

The following are the DIY Exercise – Read carefully and Do It Yourself to acquaint yourself with the learning of this book:

EXERCISE 1: CREATE A PROMPT COLLECTION

- Research different types of prompts (visual, verbal, abstract, etc.).
- Collect or create ten prompts that resonate with you.
- Categorize them based on their type and intended use (e.g., idea generation, problem-solving).
- Reflect on how each prompt can inspire creativity and innovation in different contexts.

EXERCISE 2: CRAFT YOUR PROMPTS

- Choose a theme (e.g., nature, technology, emotions).
- Create five prompts based on this theme using different techniques (e.g., open-ended questions, challenges, visual cues).
- Test these prompts on a friend or family member and observe their responses.
- Refine your prompts based on their feedback and your observations.

EXERCISE 3: BRAINSTORMING SESSION WITH PROMPTS

- Select a prompt from your collection (created in Exercise 1 or 2).
- Set a timer for 10 minutes and generate as many ideas as possible based on the prompt.
- Group similar ideas together and refine them into more detailed concepts.
- Reflect on which prompts were most effective in sparking ideas and why.

EXERCISE 4: PROMPT-FUELED CREATIVE BREAKTHROUGH

- Identify a current project where you're experiencing a creative block.
- Choose a prompt to address creative barriers (e.g., "What if you approached this problem from a different perspective?").
- Spend 15 minutes brainstorming solutions using this prompt.
- Document how the prompt helped you overcome the block and what new insights you gained.

EXERCISE 5: WRITING WITH PROMPTS

- Select a writing prompt (e.g., "Write a story that begins with someone finding

a mysterious letter").
- Write a short story, poem, or essay based on the prompt.
- Focus on originality and creativity, allowing the prompt to guide your writing.
- Share your piece with a peer for feedback and discuss how the prompt influenced your writing process.

EXERCISE 6: VISUAL STORYTELLING WITH PROMPTS

- Choose a visual prompt (e.g., a photograph, painting, or abstract image).
- Create a short comic strip or storyboard that tells a story based on the visual prompt.
- Develop characters and plot elements that align with the mood and theme of the visual.
- Reflect on how the visual prompt shaped your creative process and the narrative.

EXERCISE 7: EDUCATIONAL PROMPT CREATION

- Design three prompts that can be used in an educational setting to encourage critical thinking and skill development.
- Test these prompts with students or peers and observe their engagement and responses.
- Adjust the prompts based on feedback to enhance their effectiveness.
- Document the educational outcomes and how prompts can be integrated into various teaching methodologies.

EXERCISE 8: DIGITAL PROMPT TOOL EXPLORATION

- Research and select three digital tools or platforms for prompt generation (e.g., AI-driven prompt generators, brainstorming apps).
- Experiment with each tool by generating and using prompts in a creative project.
- Compare the ease of use, effectiveness, and features of each tool.
- Please write a brief review of each tool, highlighting how they can facilitate prompt engineering and enhance the creative process.